Date of Accession

December 78

25

Past-into-Present Series

THE WELFARE STATE

Jennifer Harris
Senior Lecturer in History
Rachel McMillan College of Education

B. T. BATSFORD LTD London

First published 1973
© Jennifer Harris 1973

Printed in Great Britain by
Redwood Press Limited, Trowbridge, Wiltshire
for the publishers
B. T. Batsford Ltd, 4 Fitzhardinge Street, London, W1H 0AH

ISBN 0 7134 1785 4

Contents

Acknowledgments 4
List of Illustrations 5

Introduction 7
1 Welfare Provision before the Eighteenth Century 8
2 Poverty in the Nineteenth Century 16
3 Public Health, 1800-1900 24
4 The Nineteenth-century Slum 29
5 School and Factory in the Nineteenth Century 34
6 Welfare Achievements by the end of the Nineteenth Century 44
7 The Beginnings of the Welfare State: Social Reform, 1906-1919 48
8 Between Two World Wars, 1919-1939 56
9 Welfare from 1939 62
10 Education, 1944-1970 69
11 Health and Housing from 1945 72
12 The Welfare State Today 78
Chronology 91
Index 94

Acknowledgments

The Author and Publisher would like to thank the following for the illustrations appearing in this book: *Architects' Journal* for fig 24; Bibliotheque Nationale for fig 1; Birmingham City Engineers and Surveyors for fig 56; the Central Office of Information for figs 57, 58, 59; Cumbernauld Development Corporation for fig 60; the Greater London Council for figs 44, 54, 62, 65; the Mansell Collection for figs 4, 23, 27, 29, 34, 42; the National Portrait Gallery for figs 16, 25; Paul Popper Ltd for fig 52; the Radio Times Hulton Picture Library for figs 6, 11, 12, 28, 33, 36, 38, 43, 45, 46, 50, 61; the University of Sussex for fig 55. They also wish to thank Oxford University Press for permission to quote the extract from *Lark Rise to Candleford* by Flora Thompson.

The Illustrations

1	Paupers at a monastery	7
2	Beggars with bowls	8
3	Begging charity	9
4	Noblewoman and sick man	10
5	Almshouses	12
6	Occupying the poor	13
7	A grammar school	14
8	Workhouse diet	15
9	Applying for poor relief	16
10	London workhouse	18
11	Hammersmith and Fulham workhouse	19
12	Outdoor relief	20
13	Warning against violence	21
14	Inmates of a casual ward	22
15	Convalescent home	23
16	Chadwick	24
17	Cholera poster	25
18	Common lodging house	26
19	Drinking fountain	27
20	London slum	28
21	Housing for the very poor	29
22	Women's lodging house	30
23	Peabody buildings, Blackfriars	31
24	Peabody buildings, Southwark	32
25	Octavia Hill	33
26	Monitorial school	35
27	Ragged school	35
28	Teaching reading	36
29	Robert Owen's school	37
30	Cotton mill	38
31	Glass-blowing factory	39
32	Dressmakers	40
33	Truants	42
34	Accommodation in sheds	45
35	Sale of stale food	45
36	Christmas in the workhouse	46
37	Slums in Leeds	47
38	Pauper children	48
39	Lloyd George	49
40	Lloyd George satirised	50
41	Pension Enquiry Officer	50
42	Labour Exchange	52
43	Election poster	55
44	Classroom in 1930s	56
45	Food distribution	58
46	Birmingham Labour Exchange	59
47	Jarrow	60
48	Liverpool slum	61
49	Bomb damage	63
50	Rationing	64
51	St Bartholomew's Hospital	65
52	Retraining centre	67
53	Child health	68
54	Comprehensive school	70
55	University of Sussex	70
56	Post-war housing scheme	73
57	Midwifery	74
58	School Medical Service	75
59	New housing, Sheffield	76
60	Cumbernauld	77
61	Unemployment	79
62	Housing development	80
63	Overcrowding	83
64	Children in sand-pit	86
65	New primary school	89

Introduction

Today we tend to take it for granted that the State will look after us from the time we are born until the time we die. We expect, as our right, a school to educate us, doctors and hospitals to care for us when we are sick, unemployment benefit when we are out of work and a pension when we are too old to earn. We also expect that the place where we live should be provided with essential services, such as a pure water supply, gas, electricity, street lighting and cleansing. We also expect to be able to enjoy parks, open spaces and the countryside.

All this of course, we pay for, indirectly, through taxation. Most of the welfare services and amenities provided by the State have been established in the twentieth century. In fact the very term 'Welfare State' was not used until the 1930s. But welfare problems such as poverty, disease, squalor and ignorance have always been in existence. We have to try to trace the origins and development of the social services. Before the nineteenth century such services did not exist. The unfortunate had to rely on help or charity from the richer members of society. Only very gradually did the State come to recognise its responsibility of providing welfare services for all.

1   Poor people arrive at the gates of a French monastery. There they are given food and medical treatment

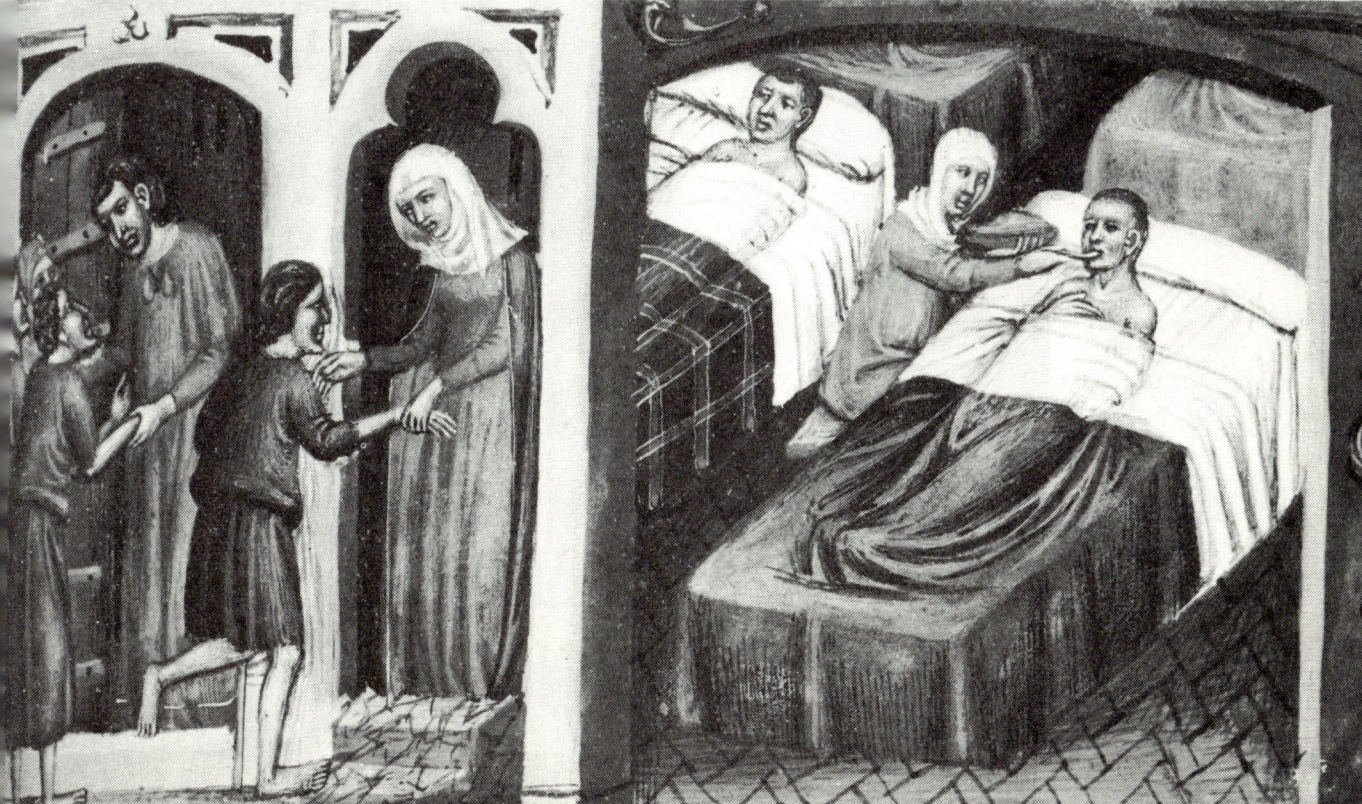

1 Welfare Provision before the Eighteenth Century

The Middle Ages

For many centuries private charity tried to cope with the problems of poverty, disease and ignorance. Helping the poor had always been seen as a Christian duty. From about the eighth century in England alms, in the form of money or food, were given by monks to the poor. Monasteries ran their own schools and hospitals, and in many areas the monastery provided work for people in the locality.

By the twelfth century, society was organised in such a way that the village itself gave a certain amount of security to ordinary people. The lord of the manor provided work for his tenants. Each person had his own place in order of importance from the lord himself, the serf who had some rights, to the slave who had none. The system depended on the social conscience of the lord of the manor and so some groups were adequately provided for, but others were almost neglected.

In mediaeval times the population expanded slowly and there was a gradual increase in the number of skilled craftsmen and merchants who worked and lived in towns. These were not subjects of a landlord and so no-one was responsible for their welfare. From the twelfth century onwards the gilds started to take over many charitable duties for townspeople. The gilds were organisations which were started originally to protect and organise different mediaeval trades. Each gild laid down regulations about length of apprenticeships served and quality of goods sold. As the gilds grew more wealthy and powerful some formed special charities which gave help to the poor. In fact many early schools were founded by gilds of merchants.

2 Here beggars are holding out their begging bowls for grain

3 A wandering beggar asks alms of a noblewoman

Many people existed upon the bare necessities of life and constantly faced the threat of starvation and fear of plague. They continued to rely on landlords or on gilds in times of hardship because there was no alternative. Parliament only took any interest in the problem of poverty when the poor seemed to threaten the security of the country. After the Black Death swept across England in 1348 one third of the population of England and Wales died. This created a vast shortage of labour. Men roamed the countryside seeking high wages for their labour. Parliament tried to stop this by passing laws against high wages and against vagrancy, but this resulted in an uprising in 1381, known as 'the Peasants' Revolt', against landowners who were trying to keep wages down. Although this rebellion failed, it was enough to worry the King and nobles about the country's security. In 1388 Parliament passed a Poor Law Act in a further attempt to prevent vagrancy. The Act stated that no person was to move from his own area without authority. But the Act did recognise that those who were incapable of earning their own living should be treated more humanely. The Act also tried to fix wages and regulate employment. For example, employers were forbidden to pay shepherds more than ten shillings a year plus board and lodging. Ploughmen were to be paid a maximum of seven shillings.

Sixteenth-century Problems
The welfare needs of the poor continued to grow. Throughout the sixteenth century various factors aggravated the situation. The monasteries had, for many centuries, provided food, clothing, schools and work for many people. In the sixteenth century, however, many monasteries were forcibly closed down. This was largely due to a quarrel between Henry VIII and the Pope, as a result of which the King had demanded that he be recognised as head of the Church in England. The closure of the monasteries caused a lot of hardship particularly in the north of England where the monasteries had played an important rôle in helping the poor.

There were other problems too: the population was increasing; prices were rising; concentration on wool production rather than grain farming meant that less men were needed to work in the countryside. The problem of vagrancy became acute as the unemployed took to the open roads. Men, women and

4 This fifteenth-century woodcut shows noblewomen looking after a sick man

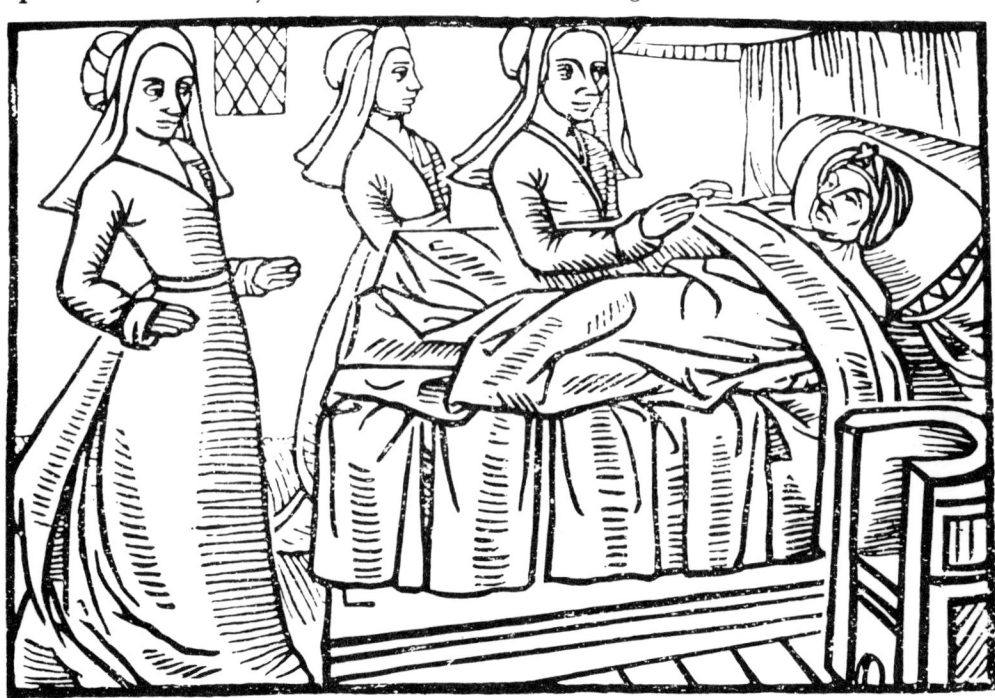

children moved from one place to another, begging and living on charity. Numbers of people from outlying areas were being forced into the towns, especially London, as there was no work available elsewhere. Provision for the old, sick and orphaned children was also becoming increasingly necessary.

The government acted only reluctantly, preferring to rely on the pattern of private charity already established in many towns. In Norwich and Bristol, groups of merchants provided aid for homeless people, educated their children and looked after the sick and elderly. But the main problem—unemployment—was unsolvable. The great majority of the population were still labourers on the land; most towns were little more than large villages and employment in them was very limited. The problem was to find work for able-bodied men.

The Statute of Artificers

In 1563 a more positive attempt was made to cope with the unemployment problem. The government passed the Statute of Artificers, which stated that men were to stay in the area where they were born. For any trade, even agriculture, a boy had to be an apprentice for seven years. Wages were to be fixed by the Justice of the Peace, who was usually the largest landowner in the locality.

The Elizabethan Poor Law Acts 1601

By the end of the reign of Elizabeth I various ideas on coping with the problem of the poor were brought together in the Poor Law Acts of 1601. By these Acts it was officially recognised that each parish would be responsible for its own poor. Each household would regularly contribute a certain sum of money—a poor rate—and each parish was to provide work for its unemployed. But although the government had passed the Acts it still depended on the community spirit of people in villages up and down the country to provide for the poor. It was a system which lasted, with additions and modifications, until 1834.

The main idea was that the poor should be given help in their own homes. There was no attempt to force them into any kind of institution or workhouse. This system was called 'outdoor relief'. Various parish officials—all of whom were amateur and unpaid—were appointed to carry out Poor Law duties. Two 'overseers of the poor' collected the poor rate from each household and distributed it amongst the needy. Pauper children, often orphans or the illegitimate, were usually lodged with a local woman who was paid about 2s 6d (12½p) a week for their upkeep. Later they would be bound out by the parish as apprentices.

But the Elizabethan Poor Law provided no radical solution since it continued to suggest that the able-bodied poor should be set to work without giving any practical suggestions on how this could be done. Although many parishes were lenient and gave help where they could, official Tudor policy still followed the mediaeval idea that a sturdy beggar should be whipped 'until his or her body be bloody', and certainly there was no central fund of money provided by the government.

5 As the charitable role of the monasteries declined individual charity became more important. These almshouses in Amersham, Buckinghamshire, were founded by William Drake in 1657

The Act of Settlement 1662

The problems of the poor were aggravated by the upheaval of the English Civil War. After this was over, a further attempt to stop vagrancy was made by the Act of Settlement of 1662. In practice this meant that any newcomer to the parish whose property was under the value of £10 a year and who was likely to need help from the parish poor rate, was to be removed to his last parish or to the place where he had been born. A complaint against newcomers had to be made to the parish authorities within forty days: later the time limit was reduced to twenty days. One can imagine how desperate families came to feel, seeking work and being hounded from parish to parish; many people spent their lives being shuttled back and forth between parishes. An added threat was transportation. As early as 1620 the City of London had sent one hundred unwanted pauper children to Virginia.

Certificate and Badging Systems

As it became increasingly obvious that men would have to leave their own parish if they were to find work the certificate practice developed. This meant that a man going to a new parish would be given a certificate from his original one which guaranteed that if he could not find work, his old parish would be responsible for him.

Another example of the growing attitude that poverty was basically a crime was the introduction in 1697 of badges for paupers. Often this could be very expensive, and the parish at Bilston, Staffs, had to pay 1s 4d (7p) in 1701 'for setting ye badge upon 8 paupers'. Paupers who refused to wear the badge were not given money. Also officials who helped paupers who refused to wear the badge were themselves liable to a £1 fine.

Private Charity in the Seventeenth Century

Although laws laid down by the State might have seemed harsh, much was being done in a very practical way by private charity. Many merchants had deep social consciences and started various charities to help the poor. Several workhouses and schools of industry were established. In Norwich over fifty charities were started in the seventeenth century. Many of these had a special function: for example, the beef and herring charities for the poor; shifts and shirts for poor men; gowns for poor women; Bibles and book charities. There was, in fact, a growing concern to educate the poor. In the later years of the seventeenth century the Charity School Movement was founded which aimed at teaching the rudiments of education to poor children to enable them to earn their living.

Social Change in the Eighteenth Century

But charitable efforts, although important, did not deal with the root causes of poverty. The need for more general welfare provision was acute even by 1700,

6 It was generally felt that the poor, if left to their own devices, would only cause trouble. This playing card from the early eighteenth century satirises the ways in which the poor were kept busy

7 St Saviour's and St Olave's Grammar Schools were founded during the reign of Elizabeth I. The original intention of the founders was to provide a free education for children in the area

yet over two hundred years were to elapse before anything on a really large scale was achieved. Meanwhile, in 1715 the House of Commons set up a committee to investigate the care of the poor in the parish of St Martin-in-the-Fields. They found that nine hundred out of twelve hundred babies born every year in the parish died. Other parishes recorded that 'no infant had lived to be apprenticed'. Problems such as these were intensified during the latter part of the eighteenth century, during which the population increased from about five million in 1750 to at least nine million by 1801.

During this period, which we call the Industrial Revolution, the English way of life was transformed. The steady migration of people from the countryside to the towns was greatly accelerated. This was made possible because improved methods of agriculture enabled farmers to produce more than was required for local needs, and so they could use the surplus to support the people of the towns. Less labourers were also needed on the land, yet the use of new machinery for factories created a demand for workers in the towns. This growth in factory employment was due in part to the discovery of steam power; inventions of new machinery; improved methods of mining to provide the coal for steam power; better roads, canals, and by 1830 railways, which enabled raw materials for industry and food for the workers to be brought into the towns. So the structure of society became predominantly a town-dwelling, manufacturing community instead of a mainly rural and agricultural community.

The system of parish care, which had been established in 1601, was really capable of operating only in small communities, and had never been of much use in towns, and the sudden expansion of the urban population brought the problem to crisis point. Although Gilbert's Act of 1782 had encouraged parishes to combine to provide workhouses, this was of little consequence, and private charity could no longer provide even a skeletal welfare service.

8 (*opposite*) A diet sheet from an early workhouse, 1723

Further reading
J. J. Bagley, *Life in Mediaeval England* (B. T. Batsford)
J. J. and A. J. Bagley, *The English Poor Law* (Macmillan)
V. E. Chancellor, *Mediaeval and Tudor Britain* (Penguin Books)
A. J. Patrick, *The Making of a Nation* (Penguin Books)
C. Wilson, *England's Apprenticeship* (Longmans)

The Bill of Fare.

	Breakfaſt.	*Dinner*	*Supper*
Sunday	Hard Bisket for the Children, Bread & Cheeſe for the old People	Buttock of Beef and Pudding	Hard Bisket for the Children, Bread & Cheeſe for the old People
Monday	Beef Broth	Cold Meat and Pudding	Bread & Cheeſe
Tueſday	Hard Bisket for the Children, Milk Porridge for the old People	Double Rands of Beef and Pudding	Bread & Butter
Wedneſday	Beef Broth	Cold Meat and Pudding	Bread & Cheeſe
Thurſday	As on Tueſday	Mouſe-piece of Beef & Peaſe Pudding	Bread & Butter
Friday	Peaſe Porridge	Cold Meat and Pudding	Bread & Cheeſe
Saturday	As on Tueſday	Thick Milk	Bread & Butter

15

2 Poverty in the Nineteenth Century

During the nineteenth century we can trace the small beginnings of social services in the fields of Poor Law, public health, housing and education on which the twentieth century was to build.

Speenhamland System

During the 1790s, famine prices had led to agricultural riots. Many farm labourers, particularly in the South of England were just not earning enough to keep themselves and their families. As a result a system was adopted in Berkshire whereby a labourer's weekly wage was supplemented according to the price of bread and the size of his family. This meant, in practice, that a labourer's wage was subsidised from the parish poor rate. The following is an extract from a report of the Berkshire Magistrates which appeared in the local newspaper, the *Reading Mercury* in 1795.

> When the loaf of flour, weighing 8lb 11oz shall cost 1s then every poor and industrious man shall have for his own support 3s weekly, either produced by his own or his family's labour, or an allowance from the poor rates; and for the support of his wife and every other of his family, 1s 6d. When the loaf shall cost 1s 4d then every poor and industrious man shall have 4s weekly for his own, and 1s 10d for the support of every other of his family. And . . . as the price of bread rises or falls . . . 3d to the man, and 1d to every other of the family, on every 1d which the loaf rise above 1s.

9 A ruined manufacturer applies to the Guardian for parish relief, 1857

This system of giving help to farm labourers from the parish poor rate rapidly spread from Berkshire into other agricultural counties. It was criticised a great deal. Many people, particularly those who had to pay the poor rate, felt that the Speenhamland System encouraged labourers to be idle as they were guaranteed a minimum wage. It was also argued that it encouraged labourers to have more children. This was hardly a valid argument as the weekly allowance for a child was insufficient for its keep. More important was the fact that some farmers may have kept down a labourer's wage knowing that he would be helped from the parish. Also Speenhamland may have damaged a labourer's morale as he knew that however hard he worked he would only be earning the same low wage. But, despite the criticisms, the Speenhamland System of outdoor relief did spread and should be seen as a humane measure adopted in years of great hardship to prevent labourers and their families from starving.

By 1830, however, much concern was felt over the increasing cost of poor relief. The poor rate had been raised from £1,500,000 in 1775 to £7,000,000 in 1832. This, of course, was largely due to the fact that the population had increased considerably and methods of industrial and agricultural production had changed. But, in 1830, landowners in the southern counties had been horrified by outbreaks of vandalism by their farm labourers. Ricks were burnt; machines were smashed by angry, hungry men who were attempting to exist on inadequate wages. Unreasonably, the whole system of outdoor relief was blamed for this.

The new Parliament, elected as a result of the 1832 Parliamentary Reform Act, felt compelled to deal with the situation. It set up a Royal Commission of enquiry into the working of the Poor Laws. Its members were nominated by the Crown and so did not necessarily represent the views of the political party in power at the time—although in practice this was often the case.

The Influence of Jeremy Bentham

Several of the Commissioners conducting the investigation were influenced by the ideas of Jeremy Bentham. Bentham had very definite ideas on the responsibilities of governments. At the time it was fashionable for the government not to interfere in people's lives at all. Bentham, however, realised that freedom for one group of people, usually the rich and privileged, to do as they wished might mean hardship for others. He felt that the government had a duty to interfere in such matters as alleviating poverty, helping people when they were ill and providing an educational system. Bentham was realistic. He was aware that people living in poverty, unable to work because of ill-health, were a burden on the State. Therefore they should be helped to keep fit and, in the long run, the country would benefit. Bentham's theories came to be known as utilitarianism—and his followers as utilitarians. They questioned the existing laws, believing that each law should serve a useful purpose and that the duties of the State should be clearly defined. Benthamism, or utilitarianism, came to mean pointing out things which needed to be done. It meant having inspectors appointed by the government, to make

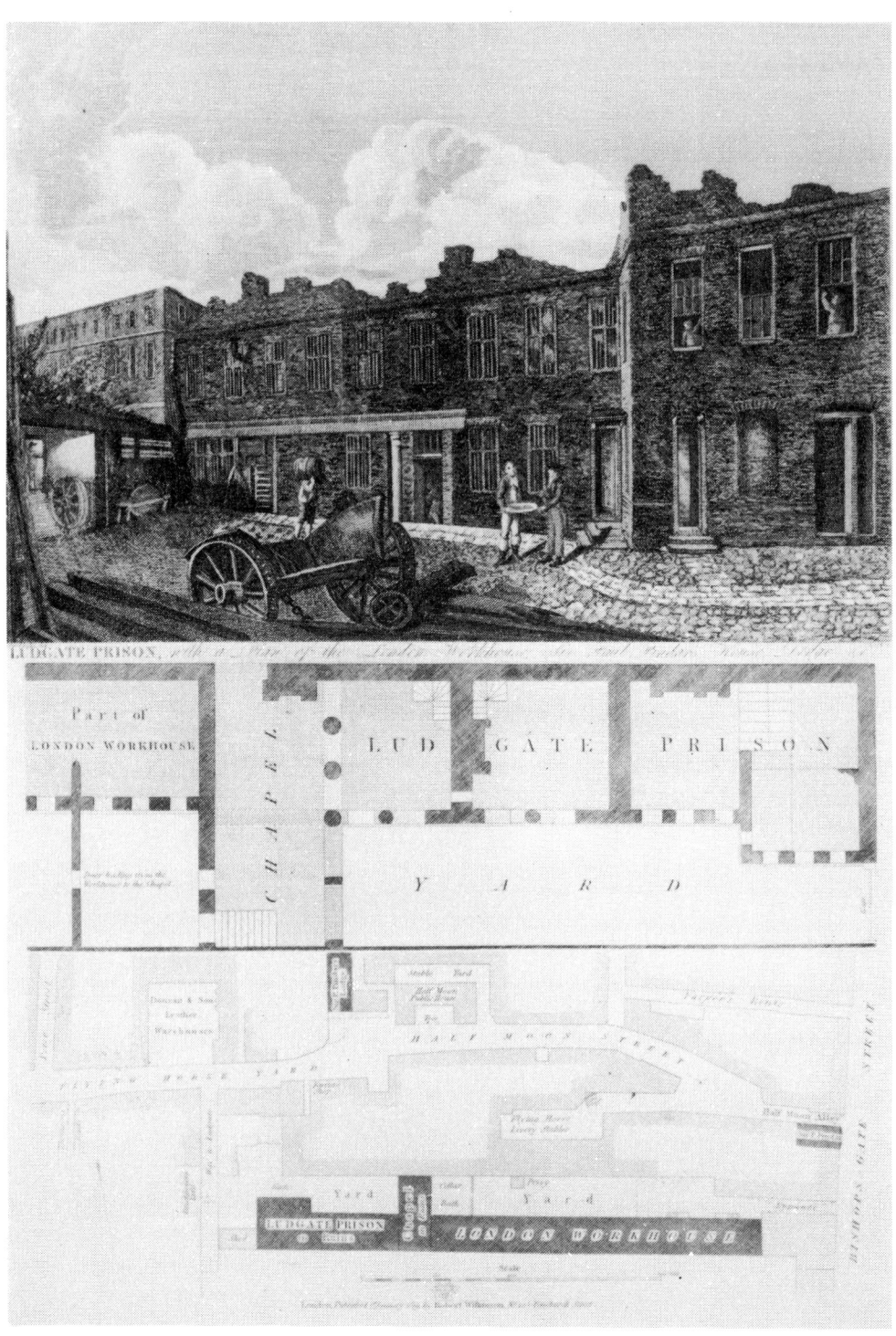

10 London workhouse, built against a ruined prison

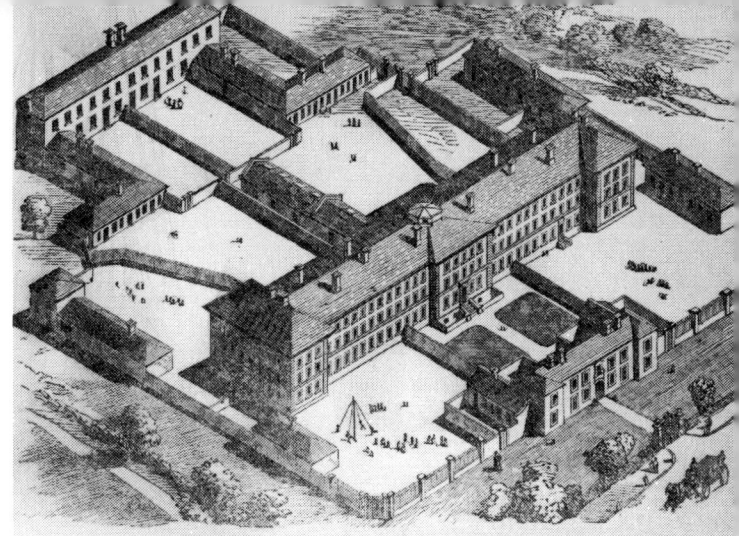

11 Under the new Poor Law the old parishes of Fulham and Hammersmith were amalgamated to provide a large general workhouse

sure that laws, which were aimed at reform, were really carried out. We can see the influence of Bentham's ideas most clearly in the fields of Poor Law, Factory Acts, sanitation and public health. Unfortunately many of Bentham's original ideas were misinterpreted and used to justify the cutting back of government expenditure.

Edwin Chadwick

Jeremy Bentham's ideas had a great influence on Edwin Chadwick who, as an Assistant Commissioner, helped in the enquiry into the Poor Laws. In fact the evidence Chadwick collected took up one third of the whole report. His early career as a journalist brought him into contact with the really poor and he became interested in the whole problem of social reform.

The general case put forward by the Poor Law Commissioners was that the whole system of poor relief was wasteful, that it demoralised the poor and needed to be improved. Certainly the report revealed that poor relief was given out in a variety of ways, many of them wasteful. The general feeling of the Commissioners was that the old and sick did not present a problem as much as the able-bodied men who were fit to work but were unable to find jobs to keep themselves and their families. Chadwick's evidence suggested that in counties where the Speenhamland System operated the numbers of able-bodied men on poor relief had actually gone up. What Chadwick did not emphasise was that the numbers of poor were increasing generally as a result of population growth and the conditions in the towns brought about by the changeover to new methods in industry.

The Poor Law Amendment Act, 1834

As well as pointing out what was wrong with the old Poor Law the Commissioners, notably Chadwick, made recommendations for its improvement. Many of these suggestions were incorporated into the Poor Law Amendment Act, 1834. Chadwick was most concerned that labouring men should get back their self-respect. So he suggested that the state of being a pauper should be made much less attractive than that of the lowest-paid worker. In other words, people

12 It was impossible to enforce the new Poor Laws everywhere. In fact outdoor relief was still given throughout the nineteenth century

who went on poor relief after 1834 would really be without hope and willing to accept anything in order to avoid starving to death.

To make sure that help was only given to those really in need it was to be administered through the workhouse. All 'outdoor' relief was to stop. The new law did not really mean to change the position for the old and sick but, in practice, the harsh treatment intended for the able-bodied pauper extended to them as well.

Workhouses were not a new idea. In fact in people's minds they were already identified with Houses of Correction which had been part of the old system. From 1834 onwards workhouses became more highly organised: parishes were grouped into unions to provide workhouses; Boards of Guardians were elected to run them; full-time officials for each workhouse were also appointed. Running the whole operation was a Central Board of three Commissioners, one of whom was Chadwick. They were to inspect the workhouses, helped by assistants.

Originally it had been intended to provide separate workhouses catering for different types of poor, but in practice there was no money for this. The mixed general workhouse of the Victorian period was regarded with fear and loathing, and many chose to starve to death rather than enter its doors. Certainly poverty in the eighteenth century and earlier had been a misfortune but during the Victorian period it became an absolute disgrace.

The Board of Guardians administered three hundred Poor Law Unions. The Office of Guardians lasted until 1930 when the work was finally taken over by Local Authorities. The Poor Law Board itself was replaced by the Local Government Board 1871 which, in 1919, became the Ministry of Health.

The Working of the Victorian Poor Law

Essentially the new Poor Law was the main form of social security available during the Victorian Period. In the early days of workhouses there were several scandals. For example, at the Andover workhouse paupers who were working on crushing bone marrow were so hungry that they were driven to eat the decaying marrow itself. At Mr Drouet's establishment in Tooting a great scandal arose after numbers of children died of cholera and the appalling conditions in which those children had lived were revealed.

Gradually matters improved after the 1860s. Within the framework of the new Poor Law various services developed. From 1842 a Medical Officer of Health was attached to the Poor Law Board, but it was not until 1864 that what were regarded as expensive medicines—cod liver oil and quinine—were given out to workhouse inmates. Because of cholera outbreaks hospitals became attached to workhouses. Eventually these hospitals were allowed to admit patients other than paupers. Another service provided by the workhouses was schools for pauper children. Ironically, in some areas there was more chance of a pauper child being educated than the child of a working labourer.

Friendly Societies

The threat of the workhouse had the undoubted effect of making those who were able to do so save through mutual insurance or Friendly Society schemes. Friendly Societies were very much a feature of mid-Victorian life, although they

Cullompton, May 14th, 1847.

At a Meeting held at the White Hart Inn, on Thursday, for the purpose of taking into consideration the distress of the Poor of this Parish, and the best means of providing for them—

It was resolved, "That it is the opinion of this Meeting that the actual wants of the Poor, more particularly in Bread Food are great, and require our sympathy and attention, to alleviate to the extent of our means; but at the same time, this Meeting deprecates the illegal and violent conduct of certain persons, in attacking the Houses of Mr. TROOD, Mr. JUSTICE, and Mr. SELLWOOD. If any repetition of violence occur, the energies of the Subscribers will be checked, the intended relief will be discontinued, and the persons requiring it, will be left to the ordinary course of the Poor Laws."

13 In their efforts to gain more food the poor attacked houses of individual magistrates. Here, the parish council of Cullompton warned that outdoor relief would stop altogether unless the attacks ceased

had been in existence for many years. They had usually begun as working men's clubs, often centred on a local inn. A group of men would agree to pay in a sum of money each week to a central fund which would entitle any one of them to a form of benefit in an emergency—for example, the expenses of a funeral or unemployment caused by sickness. Friendly Society funds were also used to help members' widows and orphans. Special acts of 1846 and 1873 gave greater legal protection to Friendly Societies and their funds. Friendly Societies also played a social rôle. Many of them organised gala days, holidays and other functions for members. Trade Unions also provided similar saving schemes which their members could join. But by 1900 for every four Friendly Society members there was only one trade unionist.

How many people did, in fact, have this insurance against the disasters of sickness, unemployment, and old age? The rough figures we have suggest that in 1815 about 8.5 per cent of the population belonged to a Friendly Society. By 1900 it was about 14.41 per cent—about half the adult male population. Benefits from the better societies were reasonable. By the end of the nineteenth century sickness pay was about 10s (50p) a week, the funeral grant was £10–£15—just about enough for a respectable funeral. The weekly contribution for this ranged from 4d to 8d (2p to 3½p). The two most important Friendly Societies were the Ancient Order of Foresters and the Manchester Unity of Oddfellows; in the 1870s these had about four million members each.

14 Henry Mayhew, a journalist, was very much concerned with the plight of London's poor. Here we see typical inmates in the casual ward of a London workhouse

15 By the end of the nineteenth century many working men had formed their own associations. As well as campaigning for improved wages, working hours and conditions, they often provided convalescent homes for their members

But contributions to Friendly Societies were usually made only by the lower-middle class upwards. The vast majority of the working class were too irregularly employed, or underemployed, to be able to afford the contributions for sickness benefit, but often they insured themselves and their families against the hated threat of a pauper funeral. Several insurance companies were in fact founded on the weekly pennies paid in for life assurance.

So by the end of the nineteenth century the harsh, deterrent nature of the 1834 Poor Law Amendment Act had been modified. In fact the Poor Law itself did provide a safety net for the very poor but all the other schemes were for people helping themselves and were certainly not provided in any way by the State.

When we examine other aspects of Victorian welfare in the field of public health, housing and education we find a similar picture of private effort and self-help with the State assuming responsibility and setting up administrative machinery for welfare services only very reluctantly.

Further reading
J. J. and A. J. Bagley, *The English Poor Law* (Macmillan)
M. Bruce, *The Coming of the Welfare State* (Batsford)
K. Dawson and P. Wall, *The Problem of Poverty* (O.U.P.)
G. Kent, *Poverty* (Batsford)
G. Taylor, *The Problem of Poverty 1660–1834* (Longmans)

3 Public Health, 1800-1900

Poverty was, of course, often caused by ill health. Disease spread at an alarming rate during the nineteenth century due to ignorance and chronic overcrowding in the industrial towns.

The Growth of Towns

Towns in the nineteenth century were growing at an alarming rate. In 1841, 48.31 per cent of the total population of England and Wales lived in towns; by 1871 this figure had risen to 65.21 per cent; by 1880 it was 70 per cent. London was the largest city in the world and was still growing as were Manchester, Birmingham, Liverpool and many others.

Such rapid urban growth caused many problems. Edwin Chadwick realised that poverty could not be dealt with solely by changing the system of poor relief. Sanitary improvements and public health also had to be considered. Again Chadwick looked at this from a practical standpoint. If health could be improved then people would not need time off work and therefore would not need poor relief. Chadwick was much impressed by the findings of Dr Southwood Smith of the London Fever Hospital. Southwood Smith's research had shown that of 77,000 cases of pauperism that he had looked at, 4,000 had been caused by poverty and not by illness. Southwood Smith's investigation had only been for London. Chadwick decided that he would look at the rest of the country.

16 Edwin Chadwick (1800–1890) was concerned about many social problems. He was responsible for endeavouring to change the system of poor relief. He also tried to improve standards of public health and housing

17 This poster gives an idea of the numbers who died from cholera, and just one of the problems caused by such an outbreak

CHOLERA.

THE DUDLEY BOARD OF HEALTH,

HEREBY GIVE NOTICE, THAT IN CONSEQUENCE OF THE

Church-yards at Dudley

Being so full, no one who has died of the **CHOLERA** will be permitted to be buried after *SUNDAY* next, (To-morrow) in either of the Burial Grounds of *St. Thomas's*, or *St. Edmund's*, in this Town.

All Persons who die from CHOLERA, must for the future be buried in the Church-yard at Nethertor

BOARD of HEALTH, DUDLEY.

Report on the Sanitary Condition of the Labouring Poor

In 1842 Chadwick produced his great work *The Report on the Sanitary Condition of the Labouring Poor*. Chadwick emphasised how much ill health was costing the nation. He suggested that piped water would reduce the danger from typhoid fever and cholera. The report was immediately a best seller and really we can regard it as the starting point of the health services. Chadwick showed very practicably, that little could be done while so many separate authorities were responsible for different aspects of town life. The water supply was in the hands of private companies. Different improvement commissions were responsible for drainage, cleansing and street lighting. Chadwick pointed out the dangerous state of the drains and emphasised the connection between dirt and disease, but he himself was unsure as to how disease spread.

The Health of Towns Commission and the Public Health Act, 1848

One effect of Chadwick's report was an enquiry made into the health of towns. As a result of a lot of pressure from people like Charles Dickens and Benjamin Disraeli, the government recommended that local Boards of Health responsible for drainage, street cleansing and water supply, should be set up. Some of the recommendations were incorporated in the Public Health Act of 1848.

The Act was passed largely because of the fear of a virulent cholera epidemic which was known to be sweeping across Asia and Europe. The Act recommended that Local Boards of Health should be set up in each town if more than one third of the ratepayers wanted this to be done, or if the number of deaths was greater than 23 per 1,000. The Boards did not have to appoint a Medical Officer of Health—they were merely allowed to do so if they wished.

Some towns had already taken action. Liverpool, for example, was one of the more go-ahead towns, possibly because it had so many children dying in infancy— 223 per 1,000 (the rate for the rest of the country was 153 per 1,000). Another town, Darlington, was also among the first to appoint a Medical Officer of Health —Dr Piper. He put forward his reasons for improving public health quite clearly.

> By the cultivation of sanitary sense we improve not only the health of the population, but also their social, moral and domestic habits. Apart from the desire to promote their welfare it is but an act of self-defence, for the rich man who lives in a comfortable and luxurious house must keep in mind that his mansion cannot be safe when the dark and filth breed pestilence beside it.

Fortunately not all had this middle-class attitude of escaping disease. Chadwick himself was very disappointed over the limited practical results of the Public Health Act. The Board of Health that was set up was very impractical. Because of opposition from interested parties who wanted to maintain the old system— old vestries, shareholders of private water companies, and slum landlords—the Board finally disappeared in 1858. In future its functions were to be divided between the Local Government Office and the new Health Department of the Privy Council.

Chadwick, who was often arrogant and very unpopular, was eventually forced to resign from the Board before it was finally disbanded. He was dissatisfied with his own achievements in the field of public health but events were to show later in the century that the work he had begun was to bear fruit.

18 Crowded, squalid conditions as in this common lodging house helped to spread infection and disease

Dr John Simon

John Simon replaced Chadwick. He was interested in the whole problem of public health and was always haunted by the wastage of human life that disease caused. Like Chadwick he saw that much disease was caused by poverty. To him, therefore, the central problem was making the poor less poor. One of the most obvious ways was to improve housing. This was difficult, as homes were the property of the land-owner and in the mid-nineteenth century it was regarded as completely wrong to interfere in what was privately owned. Even the government scarcely dared to interfere in rights of property.

Simon did not take this view. He maintained that 'the factory chimney that eclipses the light... the slaughter house that forms around itself a circle of dangerous diseases—these surely are not private, but public affairs.'

If Simon could not do much about housing he had a lot of success in other fields. Largely due to his expert team of doctors an investigation of general and specific health problems was carried out. As a result, acts were passed against the adulteration of foods, sale of poisons and for the enforcement of vaccination. Doctors were organised into professional bodies and the standard of nursing was raised.

An even more pressing force than Simon himself were the cholera epidemics. In the mid-1860s cholera struck again. As a result, in 1866 a more effective Sanitary Act was passed which required Local Authorities to take action. It was aimed at controlling the environment rather than attempting the introduction of a new public health service. It allowed the setting up of temporary isolation hospitals.

Public Health Acts, 1871–1875

Two more effective Public Health Acts were passed in 1871 and 1875. These made it compulsory for every area to have a Medical Officer of Health and a

19 Provision of drinking water was a necessity for improved public health. Often industrial cities, with the worst problems—like Liverpool—were the first to take the lead

20 In spite of the Public Health Acts, slums, such as these in Bethnal Green, still remained in the twentieth century

Sanitary Inspector. Over all was the Local Government Board which was made responsible for public health and the Poor Law. Simon himself was very disappointed about this as he had wanted a separate department or Ministry of Health. That did not come until 1919.

By the end of the nineteenth century there were positive achievements in the field of public health. It was being seen more as a problem which concerned everyone and was not just left to a few caring individuals. Vaccination against smallpox, provided free by the Poor Law Guardians from 1840, was made compulsory in workhouses after 1876. Tuberculosis was less of a killer disease although its real effects were not lessened until the discovery of new drugs in the twentieth century.

There was growing concern too for the environment, seen in the campaign for parks and open spaces. Certainly England was a safer and healthier place to live in at the end of the nineteenth century than it had been at the beginning. From 1873 the death rate had begun to drop but the mortality rate among young children was still very high.

Further reading
K. Dawson and P. Wall, *Public Health and Housing* (O.U.P.)
N. Longmate, *Alive and Well: Medicine and Public Health 1830 to the Present Day* (Penguin Books)
E. C. Midwinter, *Victorian Social Reform* (Longmans)

4 The Nineteenth-century Slum

In spite of improvements in public health one of the main problems which was still acute by the end of the nineteenth century was that of slum dwellings and housing generally. The Public Health Acts could do so much—filthy streets could be cleansed, water supplies purified; but the housing problem was much more difficult.

Houses, whatever state they were in, were worth money to their owner simply because they occupied land. If the government decided to take positive action to clear slum areas it would have to rehouse the occupants and compensate the owners.

Large property owners often left their homes in a reasonable state, but the small slum landowner often depended on rents for his own living and therefore lacked the means to improve his property.

A further problem was that housing did not keep pace with the growing population. Demand for houses exceeded supply. The census in 1861 showed that one fifth of the population in London, Bradford and Huddersfield were living at least two to a room.

Of course many houses had deteriorated into slums because of the very rapid growth of towns. Alleys, cellars and country mansions became slums almost overnight in the early decades of the nineteenth century. Nor was housing

21 This type of housing designed for the 'very poor' only catered for a small proportion of the working class who could afford to pay a regular rent

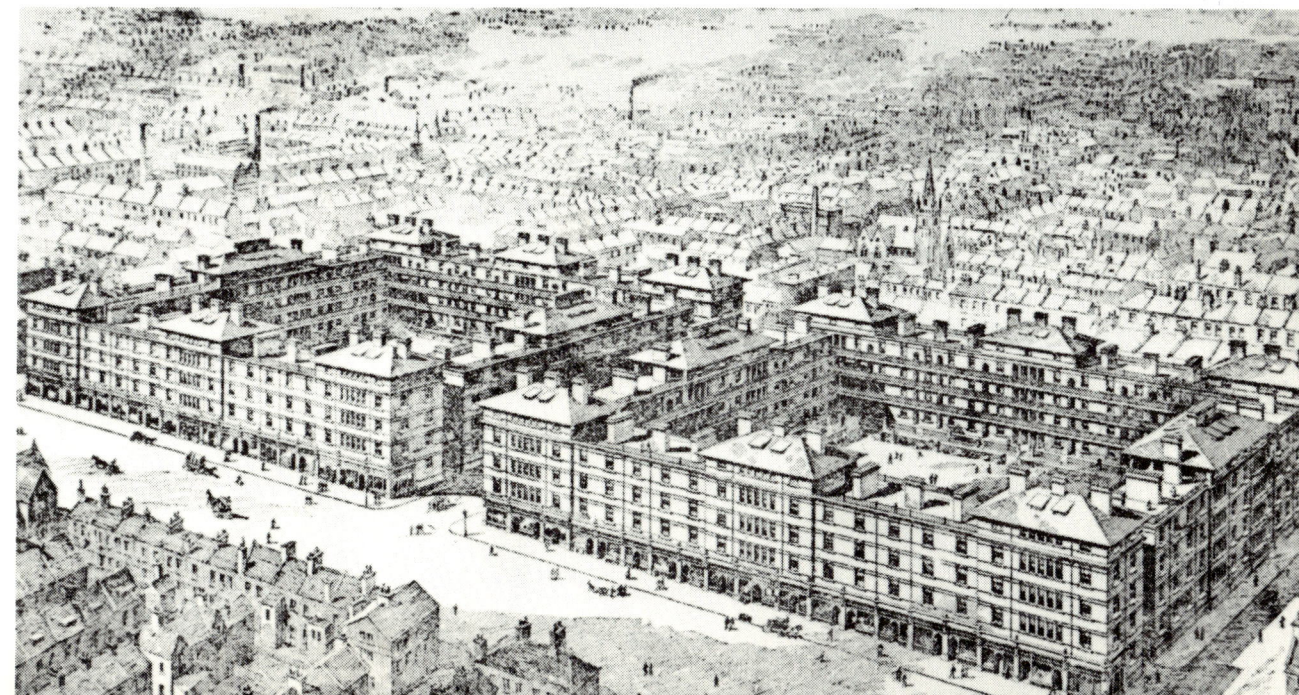

22 Many people, particularly in large cities, had no regular home. They stayed in common lodging houses, such as this one in St Giles, London, which was for women only. It cost 3d or 4d (1½p) a night to stay there

provided by firms for their workers much better. Frederick Engels, a German journalist, wrote bitter descriptions of working-class slums. One description of Manchester is particularly lurid:

> Passing along a rough bank, among slate and washing houses, one penetrates into this chaos of small one-storied huts ... kitchen, living and sleeping room all in one. In such a hole, scarcely 5ft by 6ft broad I found two beds—and such bedsteads and beds!... Everywhere before the door refuse and offal; that any sort of pavement lay underneath could not be seen but only felt, here and there with the feet. This whole collection of cattle sheds for human beings was surrounded on two sides by houses and a factory.

Of course we must remember that Engels was a Marxist who firmly believed that the working class was being exploited by their employers. But in spite of his political views there was much truth behind his description.

In fact conditions could be as bad in areas which we do not regard as industrial in the traditional mid-nineteenth century sense. For example, Brighton had its slums almost on top of the Royal Pavilion. A careful examination of the 1861 Census for a few streets covering about six acres showed that there were forty houses to an acre. (The average today for a new council estate is sixteen to an acre.) When we remember that part of this space was taken up by a timber yard, coach factory and beer cellars, the houses must indeed have been huddled together in teeming tenements.

The coming of the railway also aggravated the housing problem. The building of main line terminals such as Euston and St Pancras meant the demolition of many houses—as did the routeing of the railway lines themselves. The building of hospitals, such as St Thomas's in London and the construction of docks such as St Katherine's also meant the loss of homes. Rebuilding and rehousing schemes were half-hearted. As a result there was even greater pressure on accommodation that the working class could afford.

23 These Peabody flats in Blackfriars Road, London, were an improvement on many designs for working-class housing. At least open spaces and trees were allowed for

But we must remember that in the long run the railway did help to lessen overcrowding. Cheap fares for working men were introduced in 1883. This meant that those with regular employment could now afford to live farther away from their places of work. Before, they had either to face a long walk or live close to their place of employment.

The Attitude of the Government
The housing problem was not really acknowledged in the nineteenth century. In the second half of the century many housing acts were passed, but like the Public Health Acts, they were not compulsory. The various Nuisance Removal Acts laid down conditions which were thought to be unfit for living accommodation. Largely due to the efforts of Lord Shaftesbury the Common Lodging Houses Act was passed in 1851. Conditions in lodging houses were deplorable and the Act did at least allow them to be inspected. This was certainly a step in the right direction but it did not really achieve very much in practice.

More effective was an Act of 1868 which gave powers to Local Authorities in places with over 10,000 inhabitants to force owners to pull down or repair houses which were unfit to live in. In 1875 Local Authorities themselves were given powers to pull down slum areas. The City of Birmingham acted on this immediately by clearing a notorious slum, Corporation Street. By 1890 local councils could build their own houses, but until some form of financial aid was available from the government, little was done. Councils tended to rely on the efforts of private builders. In fact when we look at housing improvements in the nineteenth century we find it was the efforts of individuals, housing corporations and a few enlightened town councils that led the way.

24 More typical flats built by the Peabody Trust were these in Southwark

Peabody Trust and Improved Industrial Dwellings Company

The Peabody Trust was set up in 1862 to provide homes for the London poor. George Peabody's first donation was £150,000; another donation of £350,000 followed later. The Peabody Buildings were blocks of flats, and were regarded by people living at the time as model dwellings. Here is a description of Peabody Buildings in Shoreditch, written by an observer in 1866.

> Though there is nothing picturesque in these buildings the architect has done wonders for the health and comfort of the residents... the closets are numerous, private and conveniently light and spacious... closets and lavatories for men and women are separate and far apart... the ventilation of every house and room is beyond praise.... The fire grates may be too large for some families; the ovens too small; the heat of the fire may go too much up the chimney; the walls being merely whitewashed brick may wear a poorhouse or gaolhouse look; there being no supply of hot water for the baths, is almost tantamount to there being no baths at all. But tenants should not complain too much.

Probably, the rather patronising tone of the writer was due to the fact that Peabody tenants were subsidised. The Improved Industrial Dwellings Company, however, founded by Sydney Waterlow in 1863 showed that model dwellings could be provided and still make a 5 per cent profit. Many other companies were founded to build working-class housing in this way. But, of course, the rents that were charged were economic and so only workers in regular employment could afford this type of accommodation. The rest of the poor were huddled together in housing that was getting worse than ever because there was less of it.

Octavia Hill

One of the most enterprising housing improvers was Octavia Hill. She was the grand-daughter of Samuel Smiles and was very much aware that bad housing was one of the root causes of poverty. She maintained that people and houses could not be dealt with separately. In the 1860s, Octavia Hill bought up blocks of dilapidated houses, repaired them and let them out. She encouraged the tenants to be independent. Her work was not a charity as she did charge rent, but she was partly responsible for improving minimum standards. Her work also included vigorous campaigns for open spaces for slum dwellers and saving the countryside. Partly as a result of Octavia Hill's efforts the National Trust was founded in 1899.

New Towns

Some industrial firms were also concerned to provide houses for their employees. Some housing estates were built especially for this purpose: Port Sunlight model village was completed in 1887; the Quaker chocolate firm of Cadbury had built Bournville by 1895. In 1898 an important book was published called *Garden Cities of Tomorrow* by Ebenezer Howard. This inspired the building of Letchworth Garden City and, after the war, Welwyn Garden City.

Not much was done to improve housing in rural districts, but in the towns there was some progress. Better housing and town planning were being recognised as necessary when the First World War broke out and interrupted many schemes.

Further reading
A. Briggs, *Victorian Cities* (Penguin)
K. Dawson and P. Wall, *Public Health and Housing* (O.U.P.)
H. J. Dyos, *Victorian Suburb* (Leicester University Press)
T. Hastie, *Home Life* (Batsford)
S. Healy, *Town Life* (Batsford)

25 Octavia Hill (1838–1912) felt strongly about the lack of adequate housing. She campaigned vigorously for improved housing and open spaces for working people

5 School and Factory in the Nineteenth Century

By 1830, there were more children living in the expanding towns than in the countryside. Most children had little chance of any kind of education as they were required to work in factories, mines and workshops of all kinds. As a result, such educational opportunity that existed was very much on a part-time basis provided by concerned individuals. Only gradually, as the working day was shortened and there was less demand for child labour, did the government recognise its responsibility for providing schools for everyone.

The Voluntary Societies

Before 1870 education was very much a privilege. It was available at grammar and public schools and university for those who could pay. For the great mass of children a very rudimentary type of education was provided by two religious societies, the non-conformist British and Foreign Society and the Anglican National Society. The schools run by the societies concentrated on teaching the 'three R's'—reading, writing and arithmetic. There was also a strong religious element in the education provided. Discipline was very strict; learning was 'by rote'; teaching methods were very formal.

The Monitorial System

In order to cope with growing numbers of children, the voluntary schools made use of the monitorial system. By this a monitor, or older pupil, would teach a group of younger children what he had learnt. This meant that a teacher could cope with a large number of children. Dictation and round-the-class reading were part of the daily curriculum, so was writing the alphabet on a slate. Children were rewarded for good work and behaviour. Bad behaviour was punished often by hands or legs being tied together, or the child was sent to stand in a corner. In one school a child was even put in a basket on the school roof.

In 1833 the voluntary schools were given a grant of £33,000. This amount increased each succeeding year. Most of the voluntary schools were, in fact, run by the National Society which between 1839 and 1850 received 80 per cent of the government grant to education.

Hazelwood School, Birmingham

Some schools were run on very functional, utilitarian lines. The aim was that each minute of the child's day should be occupied. At Hazelwood School, Birmingham, the bell rang 250 times a day. Children got up at 6 a.m., classes started at 7.20 a.m. although breakfast was not until 9.05 a.m.

26 The monitorial system in action. Monitors from each class are being instructed by their teacher. This is the Lancastrian Free School, in Severn Street, Birmingham, founded in 1809, for 400 boys

27 Ragged schools existed for the very poor. (The voluntary schools tended to cater for the more respectable end of the working class.) Often work done in ragged schools was sold for profit

28 In a Lambeth ragged school children are taught to read

The principles of a school, such as Hazelwood, are reflected in contemporary literature. This comes out very clearly in the opening paragraph of *Hard Times* by Charles Dickens; the speaker felt that facts alone were what children should be taught and this was his advice.

What I want is Facts. Teach these boys and girls nothing but Facts. Facts alone are wanted in life. Plant nothing else, and root out everything else. You can only form the minds of reasoning animals upon Facts; nothing else will ever be of any service to them.

In many ways these expanding schools can be compared with growing factories and the new workhouses. Numbers were large, discipline was vigorous and the halls were huge and draughty. It is interesting that the early factories originally consisted of barn-like buildings with workshops off them. Many schools were originally vast halls with tiered seating and galleries for different classes. Later the idea of having classrooms leading off halls was developed.

Factory Reforms
In fact the growing pressure on Parliament to provide a national system of basic elementary education follows a similar pattern to the demands for laws which aimed at stopping children from being employed in factories and mines. As early as 1796 a group of doctors in Manchester had pointed out that children who were herded into factories 'formed a seedbed for infectious diseases'.

Health and Morals of Apprentices Act
In 1802 Sir Robert Peel led a campaign to protect pauper children who were sent to work in industrial areas. He wanted to limit hours worked by young

apprentices to twelve a day. He also wanted reasonable living and working conditions to be provided for them. What Peel, as a factory owner, had been trying to do was to enforce on all employees the reasonable conditions provided by the most humane millowners for their apprentices. A further Act (1819) stated that no child under nine should be employed in textile mills but this was difficult to carry out in practice. Magistrates were supposed to do the job, but many of them were millowners themselves. Also, there was no legal way, before the compulsory registration of births, marriages and deaths in 1837, of telling whether a child had reached the age of nine.

By 1831 however, women and young people in textile mills formed the largest single group of workers. It was essential that they should receive some form of protection. An act alone was not enough; what was needed was some way of making sure that it could be enforced.

After a long campaign a Factory Act was passed in 1833. Evidence of exploitation had been gathered by a Royal Commission. Three central Commissioners, helped out by local Commissioners, went round many industrial areas with long questionnaires. Young children were brought before the Commissioners and told harrowing tales of the long hours they worked, often in appalling conditions.

As a result of the Act, hours of work for young persons of 13 to 18 years were restricted to twelve a day, and eight hours for 9 to 13 years olds. These had to be worked in the daytime only. In fact this meant that adult working hours were reduced in cotton, woollen and linen mills because the machines could not be operated without child labour. Children under nine were not to be employed at all. Factory owners were also to provide two hours schooling a day.

There was still the problem, however, of making sure that the Act worked. At first only four Inspectors were appointed to supervise all textile concerns. Eventually more Inspectors were appointed after one, Robert Rickards, died of overwork as his area was the whole of the northern textile district. The Inspectors were given a gentleman's salary of £1,000 a year. It attracted able and educated men.

The main difficulty was not in enforcing the minimum age of nine years, but the eight-hour day for children between nine and thirteen years. Parents wanted higher wages for a fuller day and therefore would often lie about their child's

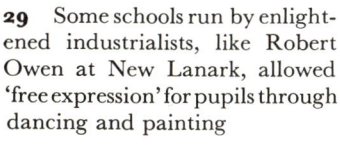

29 Some schools run by enlightened industrialists, like Robert Owen at New Lanark, allowed 'free expression' for pupils through dancing and painting

age. Children themselves often disliked the factory school and adult workers in factories needed children's assistance to enable them to do their work, so children of ten, eleven and twelve often became thirteen 'overnight'. It seemed that the factory workers were trying to defeat the factory laws.

The Act also meant that factory owners had to do a lot more paperwork. Time, books, later a register, had to be kept showing the hours which the machinery was worked. Children entering the mill had to bring a certificate showing they were nine years old. They also had to bring a weekly certificate showing that they had been at school for at least twelve hours in the previous week. Then another certificate was required when the child went on to a twelve-hour day at thirteen years old.

The educational provision was also very difficult to enforce. Some millowners provided good schools. Most, however, resented having to provide any. The local day schools naturally did not like having children coming in for lessons at odd hours. As a result too many factory schools were often held in sheds or out-houses. Often the school was just used as a place for minding children rather than educating them.

1844 Factory Act

Obviously another Act was necessary. Another Parliamentary Committee inquired into the workings of the earlier Act. Finally the minimum age of eight years for children working was decided on. They were not to work more than seven hours a day. Night shift work was forbidden for children and women.

The Ten Hours Act, 1847

By 1847 a ten-hour working day was established for women and young people. However, factory owners got round this by breaking up the day so that women and young workers had two-hour gaps from work but were in fact kept hanging around the factory for a much longer period than ten hours. The plight of these young workers was taken up by Lord Ashley, later Lord Shaftesbury, and others who felt young people should have their evenings free so that they could go to school.

30 Work in the cotton mills. Women and young girls are engaged in the mechanical processes of carding, drawing and roving

31 The Factories and Mines Act did not apply to all trades. Long hours were still worked in glass-blowing factories

There was a special court case over the whole matter but the judges decided that factory owners were not, in fact, acting illegally by operating this type of shift system. Therefore the only way around the whole issue was another law. Lord Ashley worked hard for this in Parliament. Many members of the 'Ten Hours Movement'—the campaign for a ten-hour working day—felt that the new act was a betrayal as it was a compromise. What emerged was a ten-and-a-half-hour working day—but the shift or relay system was forbidden.

So by 1852 hours for children and young people in cotton and worsted mills had been very substantially reduced. As a result the working hours of adults had also been shortened.

Mines Act, 1842

People had also been working in other areas to get Parliament to improve conditions and reduce working hours. Lord Ashley, in 1841, had persuaded the government to set up a 'Royal Commission on the Labour of Children in Mines and Colleries and other Unregulated Trades'. The first report came out in 1842. What it revealed caused a sensation: women and children spent many hours underground; they had to crawl along on their hands and knees dragging heavy trucks; they had to haul buckets up to the surface. They were grossly ill-treated by the miners themselves and there were many horrific accidents. The report was illustrated with pictures of workers underground and working conditions. It certainly had the required effect. In 1842 a Mines Act was passed which forbade the employment underground of women and girls and of boys under ten. An Inspector of Mines was appointed in an effort to see that the law was carried out.

The other report brought out by the same Commission concerned the working hours of children in calico printing. It was suggested that there should either be a compulsory education of children before they were employed or that education should be provided during slack seasons. This report was largely ignored, but it is important as it did emphasise the growing pressure on the State to do something positive about working hours, conditions and education of children.

32 Dressmaking was not a regulated trade. Girls had to work very long hours to complete orders—often until 1 am

School Inspectors

Of course, limiting the hours that children worked in factories meant that increasing numbers of them were now free to be educated. The idea of inspectors, first used in the factories, was also applied to the elementary school system, if the patchy arrangement made for the education of working-class children before 1870 could be so called. During the 1840s and 1850s various efforts were made to improve conditions in schools and also the quality of the teaching. As we have seen the State was paying out grants to the voluntary schools' societies from 1833. In the 1840s the State sent round its own inspectors—Her Majesty's Inspectors. When the Inspectors first got their instructions it was stressed that they existed 'to provide the promoters of such efforts with the opportunity of learning improvements in the apparatus and internal arrangement of schools, in school management and discipline, and in the methods of teaching'.

The Inspectors were chosen with great care, the reports they wrote were published in full and did a lot to encourage improved teaching and general interest in education. It was through the efforts of the Inspectors that the monitorial system was abolished and class teaching introduced. But to abandon monitors created a shortage of teachers. This problem was largely solved by the efforts of Sir James Kay Shuttleworth, who introduced the pupil teacher scheme.

Pupil Teacher System

In 1846 a scheme was drawn up which created a pupil teacher system. Really this was similar to an apprenticeship scheme. Children over thirteen years who wanted to teach could be apprenticed to a teacher for five years. During that time they could do some teaching themselves and also be instructed by the teacher. At the end of each year their work was examined by an HMI and, if satisfactory, both teacher and pupil would get a grant. There were special Queen's Scholarships available for some pupil teachers to go on to a training college.

As a result of James Kay Shuttleworth's scheme, elementary school teaching came to be regarded as a fairly secure occupation. The number and quality of recruits improved. Certainly it provided a career for gifted working-class children.

The Newcastle Commission and Payment by Results

In 1858 the government decided to investigate the state of elementary education. What they found did not please them. The members of the Commission who were sent round to investigate maintained that many children did not even learn to read and write in school. Others, they felt, were being deliberately encouraged by their teachers to study languages and science—accomplishments which the Commissioners thought were useless to working-class children! The Commissioners wanted to prevent this in the future and so devised a 'payment by results' system which had administrative as well as educational attractions.

Robert Lowe, then Vice-President of the Committee of the Council on Education, reorganised the whole system of the government grant to the voluntary schools. In the Revised Code, as it came to be called, a grant of 12s (60p) was given per child: 4s (20p) for attendance, 8s (40p) for his performance in 'the three Rs', tested at yearly intervals. The examinations were conducted in standards; each child was expected to move up a standard each year.

James Kay Shuttleworth and other HMIs bitterly opposed this system which they felt was very much a backward step. They felt that it would encourage teachers merely to concentrate on teaching the mechanics of reading, writing and arithmetic and neglect the wider aspects of education. In fact, by the mid-1860s the outlook for a State system of education indeed seemed gloomy. The amount of the government grant had actually gone down; standards had been raised, but the Revised Code had set definite limits. There was still very much the idea that the great mass of children should not be encouraged to move out of their social class. Yet in spite of the apparent lack of progress in setting up a State system of education, this was achieved by the Education Act of 1870. Why was this? Several explanations have been suggested.

In 1867 more people were given the right to vote. Did this mean that the government was now concerned about the possibility of large numbers of voters who could not read or write? It hardly seems likely that Parliament would extend the vote and then worry about the suitability of new voters. Nor can we really accept the suggestion that the new voters would suddenly demand government action on education.

Another explanation put forward is that the government was concerned about the effects of foreign competition on English industries. But from the early nineteenth century, various people had pointed to the educational advances on the continent to emphasise the weakness within the English educational system.

Possibly we can explain the 1870 Act by the fact that there were increasing numbers of children around who were no longer needed to work in factories and workshops. Partly they were excluded by law, but also the machines themselves were becoming too complicated to be worked by children.

Another more down to earth reason was that the voluntary societies were finding it increasingly difficult to run their schools because of rising costs. There had always been bitter rivalry between the British and Foreign Society and the National Society. This alone was to make the actual passing of any general education act very difficult. It was finally passed in 1870. At last the State was committed to provide a national system of elementary schools. The Act created a new type of Local Authority to run the new schools—the School Board. School Boards were to be elected by ratepayers and the schools were to be financed from the rates. The voluntary schools were to be used in places where they existed, but if there were no school at all then the School Board had to find one. If religion was taught then it had to be simple Bible teaching with no denominational bias.

33 School children truanting from school are caught by a London School Board Inspector

But there were still problems—school attendance was but one. Although the State had provided an elementary system of education, attendance was not made compulsory until 1880. Schools were not free until 1891.

Gradually new teaching methods were introduced. 'Payment by results' slowly disappeared. Physical exercise was introduced into the curriculum. Educational visits were encouraged. Gradually it became possible for some pupils to go beyond standard 6—the highest standard of the elementary school—to higher-grade schools. But these children were only a minority and tended to be the children of skilled workers. In reality, education for working-class children at the end of the nineteenth century was not very much different in type than it had been at the beginning. The main difference was that it was no longer dependent on Factory Acts.

Secondary Education

Already by 1902, concern was again being felt over education. Much of the concern was political and was felt against School Boards, some of which in the larger cities were very powerful indeed. Other small rural Boards were often too small and had insufficient money from the rates to run their schools.

By the 1902 Act, School Boards were abolished and also the higher grade schools. The School Boards were replaced by Local Education Authorities. These were given responsibility for all schooling and if they wished, could provide free secondary education. Technically, therefore, it was possible for a poor child to progress from elementary school, through secondary school and by aid of scholarships, to university. It was, however, extremely unlikely that this would happen except to a very few.

The new Local Authority secondary schools were modelled on the old grammar schools—expensive uniform, classical curriculum. The extra expense of such schooling often put the secondary school beyond the reach of most working-class children.

Further reading
K. Dawson and P. Wall, *Education* (O.U.P.)
K. Dawson and P. Wall, *Factory Reform* (O.U.P.)
U. Henriques, *The Early Factory Acts and their Enforcements* (Historical Association)
P. Speed, *Learning and Teaching in Victorian Times* (Longmans)
G. Sutherland, *Elementary Education in the Nineteenth Century* (Historical Association)

6 Welfare Achievements by the end of the Nineteenth Century

What had been achieved in terms of welfare services by the end of the nineteenth century? Certainly England at the end of the century was a better place for the mass of people to live in than it had been in 1800. There had been a complete change in the attitude of the government during this period. At the beginning it had not been thought necessary or desirable that the State should interfere in people's lives in any way; gradually, however, through the efforts of individuals the government had been made aware of its responsibility to act in such fields as coping with the poor, providing some kind of public health service and an educational system. In other words the State was gradually assuming collective responsibility for the welfare of the individual.

We have to ask why this happened. Probably general factors such as population growth, industrialisation and the growth of towns created problems which, although they had existed before, had expanded dramatically. The extension of the right to vote—by the end of the century to all adult males over 21 years, the growth of Trade Unions with their demand for regulated hours, better wages and working conditions were also important.

But in spite of some progress, great numbers of people still lived in acute poverty; it is ironic that during the last part of the century when England was busy consolidating and extending an Empire abroad, so much remained to be done at home. Certainly the Boer War in South Africa (1899–1902) interrupted very severely programmes of social reform. Investigations carried out by Commissions and individuals at the turn of the century show vast areas of need. It was partly because of these revelations together with the growth of Trade Unions for unskilled labours to exert pressure on the government, a socialist political party to express working-class grievances and exert pressure within the government, and the example of social reform in Germany that led to a definite policy of social welfare being introduced in the first decade of the twentieth century.

University Settlements
In the last part of the nineteenth century there was certainly a stirring of conscience among the comfortably-off middle and upper classes. The rich were feeling a sense of moral obligation to help the poor. Several young men at Oxford University were influenced by the teaching of T. H. Green who strongly believed that all citizens should have the right to grow in freedom. This had a practical result in the formation of a settlement in the East End of London—St Jude's,

34 Despite some improvements in social welfare many people were still homeless. In 1888 these sheds in Whitechapel were filled with men, women and children who had nowhere else to go and London parks were full of homeless people

Whitechapel. In 1884 Toynbee Hall was founded. The idea of this was that earnest young men from university could have the opportunity to live among the poor where they could organise help for the local community and draw public attention to its needs. In many ways the settlements and Toynbee Hall in particular, became a sort of training ground for future politicians who were interested in social reform.

Charles Booth

Charles Booth, a wealthy Liverpool shipowner, settled in London in the 1870s and was determined to find out the cause and effect of poverty. He studied the census returns to get some idea of the distribution of poverty, and was very much influenced by the findings of the Social Democratic Federation who had made a survey of working-class wages, which revealed that few men could lead a healthy existence on what they earned.

Booth made a detailed examination of the East End and Central London by means of a house to house survey. This took so much time that he looked at the rest of London street by street. Altogether Booth, with his team of dedicated investigators, covered more than one million families. He did not try to explain or offer remedies for what he found. What he wanted was an 'instantaneous picture'. This he achieved.

35 Waiting for shopkeepers to distribute unsaleable stale food in London, 1822

Booth's evidence revealed that one-third of the working class were living below the poverty line of £1 a week. One-third of his million lived in overcrowded conditions—two or three to a room. He found that where poverty was most acute the death rate was highest. He noticed too the connexion between old age and poverty. Also he saw how poverty seemed endemic where men were employed in intermittent or casual work.

The survey made an impact in all circles. It showed that charity as a means of helping the poor was virtually useless. Booth, like Sir John Simon, wanted to see the poor less poor and felt strongly that the whole community should be made responsible. It is possible that had the Boer War not intervened, some form of social welfare might have been introduced. The idea of old age pensions, such as had been introduced into Germany in the 1880s, had already been discussed in Parliament, but the outbreak of war prevented any positive action from being taken.

Seebohm Rowntree

Charles Booth had investigated conditions in London but it could be argued that London was not typical and therefore the findings of the survey could not be applied to the rest of the country. Another enquiry was made by Seebohm

36 Workhouses had not changed much in character by 1900. Old people hated being institutionalised. Even the Christmas celebrations do not disguise the general regimentation

37 Slum houses, such as these in Leeds, were typical of those found in many cities

Rowntree into conditions in York in 1899 and the results were published in 1901. (Later Rowntree wrote further surveys, in 1936 *Poverty and Progress*, and again in 1950 *Poverty and the Welfare State*.)

Rowntree's 1899 investigation showed how conditions in the country town of York could be compared with Booth's findings in London. His survey showed that 28 per cent of the population of York lived below the poverty line. Again among the poor there seemed to be more ill-health and a higher death rate.

Rowntree looked particularly at the condition of children. He found that at thirteen, the age for leaving school, boys from the poorest background were on average 11 lbs lighter and $3\frac{1}{2}$ ins shorter than boys from more prosperous homes of the working class.

Rowntree largely confirmed Booth's findings. This was especially significant as medical authorities had found that they had had to reject many recruits for the Boer War as physically unfit. It did seem, therefore, that a lot of man-power was being wasted—a fact that was to influence governments of the early twentieth century considerably.

Further reading
A. M. Newth, *Britain and the World 1789–1901* (Penguin)
Seebohm Rowntree, *Poverty: A Study of Town Life* (Longmans)
R. S. Sayers, *A History of Economic Change in England 1880–1939* (O.U.P.)

7 The Beginnings of the Welfare State: Social Reform 1906-1919

When the Liberal government was elected in 1906 it had no immediate plans for widespread social reform—but it had inherited a new Education Act, establishing the beginning of State secondary education, from the Tory government and also a Commission that had been set up to look into the working of the Poor Law.

The Poor Law Commission, 1905-1909

This was really a grand inquiry once again into the state of the nation's poor. Members of the Commission included Octavia Hill, Charles Booth and Beatrice Webb. There was strong disagreement among the members of the Commission and as a result there were two reports.

Most of the members felt that the Poor Law Guardians had served their purpose and should go. The majority report wanted Local Authorities to take over the running of the Poor Law, and the name changed to Public Assistance. What was important was the recognition, finally, that different aspects of poverty should be treated in different ways—outdoor relief for the unemployed, medical aid, better co-ordination of private charity which could work alongside the Public Assistance Committees.

The minority report was largely the work of Sidney and Beatrice Webb, both ardent socialists. They insisted that it was complete destitution that was the problem. In other words, many people were so poor that they would never be able to escape from poverty. The Webbs made practical suggestions for doing something about this: Labour Exchanges to help the unemployed, insurance against sickness and unemployment.

The inquiry did have an important influence on ideas about welfare which were circulating in these years before the outbreak of war in 1914. The Liberal

38 These children in Lambeth show the need for adequate food and housing at the end of the nineteenth century

39 David Lloyd George (1863–1945) cared very deeply about social reform. Largely through his efforts old age pensions, unemployment insurance schemes and national health insurance, were started

government 1906–1914 was to introduce important measures on which the Welfare State as we know it was to be built. In some respects this early action was consolidating what the Victorians had begun in a small way. What was new, however, was the growing acceptance of the idea that poverty was not a crime, that everyone in need had a right to be helped by the State. We can see this changing attitude best by examining the new measures which benefited the old, the unemployed, the sick and children.

David Lloyd George

Significantly, early welfare measures were tied up almost inextricably with political events and personalities. David Lloyd George was one of the most dynamic. He was very much aware that 'incalculable wealth and undesirable poverty' dwelt side by side and was determined to do something about it. As Chancellor of the Exchequer he introduced a special budget to pay for the reforms he wanted to see introduced.

Old Age Pensions

That old age caused acute poverty had been recognised for some time. As we have seen some people were able to save money to use in their old age through Friendly Society and Trade Union schemes, but the great majority had no such security. State aid was obviously necessary. The practical problem, however, was whether people should contribute towards a pension during their working lives or whether they should just be given it from general taxation.

Pensions had already been introduced in Germany, and Lloyd George paid a visit there to see how the scheme worked. Several suggestions to introduce pensions into England had already been made in the 1880s and 1890s. Charles Booth had pointed out that a pension 'would lift from very many old hearts the fear of the workhouse at the last'.

In 1908, largely as a result of the efforts of Lloyd George, pensions were introduced into England. They were given as of right—in other words people did not have to prove that they were destitute. All people over the age of 70 whose

40 (*left*) This contemporary cartoon satirises Lloyd George's efforts to set up a pension fund for old people

THE PHILANTHROPIC HIGHWAYMAN.
Mr. Lloyd George. "*I'll make 'em pity the aged poor!*"

41 (*below*) A Pension Enquiry Officer visits an old person

SWEET MEMORIES.
Pension Enquiry Officer. "Have you ever been in the hands of the police?"
Applicant. "Well—er—sir, you see I used to be a cook! Girls will be girls! Besides, it was a good many years ago, and he was a sergeant!"

income was not more than £31 a year were to be given 5s (25p) a week. It was certainly not very much, but at least it was a start. Asquith, the Prime Minister, had estimated that £6 million per annum would cover the cost, but in 1909–1910 the scheme was already costing £8 million; by 1913 it was £12 million. This showed that there were a lot more old people in need than had been thought.

The pensions were paid out to old people through their local Post Office. Here is an extract from a novel *Lark Rise to Candleford* by Flora Thompson describing old people's reactions to the new pensions.

> When the Old Age Pensions began, life was transformed for such aged cottagers. They were relieved of anxiety. They were suddenly rich. Independent for life! At first when they went to the Post Office to draw it, tears of gratitude would run down the cheeks of some and they would say as they picked up their money, 'God bless that Lord George!' (for they could not believe one so powerful and munificent could be a plain 'Mr') 'and God bless you miss!' and there were flowers from their garden and apples from their trees for the girl who merely handed them the money.

Unemployment

Another cause of poverty was unemployment. Already employers had been made liable to pay out for injuries caused to employees when they were at work. But the major problem still remained—that jobs were not really organised. Men often found themselves in areas where there was no work available. William Beveridge, who had joined the Board of Trade under Winston Churchill, felt that this problem could be solved by Labour Exchanges, an idea which had been suggested by the Minority Report on the Poor Law. Labour Exchanges were set up in 1910 and Beveridge was appointed as Director for the whole country.

Labour Exchanges represented a most important step forward. For the first time the government had set up a department which was aimed at providing a service to help people to find jobs. Initially the Labour Exchanges were regarded with suspicion. Many people felt that really they were just something to do with the workhouse. At first they were just used by skilled men, but gradually, unskilled men came to use them. Also, the Exchanges were useful as later they did provide places where unemployment benefit could be paid out.

We have already seen that some workers were able to protect themselves against the risk of unemployment through Friendly Society, Trade Union and Insurance Company schemes. But the vast majority of families were unable to do this. Lloyd George was anxious that the government should introduce a scheme which would benefit more people.

The plan finally adopted in England was based on that already in use in Germany. The Insurance fund was built up by the worker and employer each paying $2\frac{1}{2}$d while the State paid a further 3d (about $1\frac{1}{2}$p). In return for his contribution a workman would then be guaranteed 7s (35p) a week when he was

42 Labour Exchanges, by 1910, came to be used by people from all social classes who were out of work

unemployed. He qualified for one week of benefit for each five contributions paid. The maximum amount of unemployment pay any man could draw was fifteen weeks. Special cards were used and stamps issued. These were kept by the employer and given back to a worker when he wanted to change his job.

The Insurance scheme was very experimental. It only applied to a small number of trades—mostly those with low wages and irregular employment, for example, building, mechanical engineering, shipbuilders. No one regarded it as the answer to unemployment, but it was a start and the whole idea of unemployment insurance later extended to family allowances and benefits for dependants.

National Health Insurance, 1911
Lloyd George, besides caring about the old and unemployed, was well aware, as many nineteenth-century reformers had been, that ill-health was a cause of poverty. Lloyd George had been most impressed by the health service he had seen working in Germany. He was aware that something drastic needed to be

done in England. He realised that in spite of schemes operating through Friendly Societies, Industrial Insurance and the Charity Organisation Society, these were not enough. Problems of health, particularly for the poor living in towns, had not been solved. Tuberculosis was still the killer disease and many people died because they could not afford medical aid.

The scheme Lloyd George introduced could be operated through Friendly Societies and Trade Unions. Everyone earning less than £160 a year (most of the working population) had to pay into the scheme. Each week 4d (about 2p) was collected from the employee, 3d from the employer and the State contributed 2d. To the worker this scheme seemed very fair. He felt as if he were, in fact, getting '5d for 4d'.

The contributions entitled a man to 10s (50p) a week when he was sick. It also included a maternity grant of 30s (£1.50). It also included the right to medical attention and medicine. The main drawback was that it was only the father of a family or working man who benefited. When wives and children were ill, their medical treatment still had to be paid for.

At first there was great opposition from doctors to the Health Insurance Act, who were afraid that they might lose some of their income, and did not want interference in their practices. Eventually they agreed to a scheme whereby they formed panels which their patients joined. Also doctors were allowed to treat private patients who paid for their treatment in full.

The National Insurance Act eventually led to the creation of two new government Ministries—the Ministry of Labour, set up during the First World War in 1916 and the Ministry of Health in 1919. The Act also focused attention on a problem which still faces the Welfare State today. How does the State provide for those really in need? If everything is provided as of right then this could discourage saving. It has also been argued that public money would be wasted on those who were wealthy enough not to need a free health service or unemployment benefit.

Children

During the beginning of this century, concern was felt about the health of children. It was realised that they were a good investment particularly as the birthrate was falling. There was quite a real threat for the future of there being fewer children around, and an ageing population. Many children in the early twentieth century did not survive the first year of infancy. Many of those who did live were undernourished and physically unfit. Often this was due to poverty and a low standard of housing.

In 1906 a conference was held in London to consider the problem of the high infant death rate. This led to the first steps being taken towards improving the health of children. 'Schools for Mothers', later Infant Welfare Centres, were set up. Mothers were made aware of the value of clean milk and food for their babies. Clean milk depôts had already been established at St Helens and Liverpool and gradually these spread over the whole country. Local Authorities were encouraged to have their own health visitors. By 1915 it was made compulsory for all births to be notified to the Local Authority so that at least they could know where help was likely to be needed. Also special maternity hospitals were built. These helped to cut down the infant death rate. The maternity grant established by the Health Insurance scheme, although inadequate to cover the cost of a new baby, was at least something.

Certainly this care for mothers and young babies did have positive results. In 1899, 163 babies in every 1,000 died, by 1912 this number had fallen to 93. The problem of women dying in childbirth still remained.

Child Welfare
The poor physique of children at school was still causing concern. It was found by teachers, that many children were under-nourished. Their main meal a day often consisted of bread and jam. Already many Local Authorities were providing midday meals for school children. In 1906 they were given permission by the School Meals Act to use ½d from the rates for this purpose. By 1910, ninety-six authorities were providing school meals. The number of children having meals had risen from less than three million to over nine million.

In 1907 another very important step forward was taken when a personal health service was established in schools. The eyes, ears and teeth of school children could now be inspected regularly. The only drawback was that parents often ignored advice given by the school Medical Officer to take their children to the doctor—often because they could not afford to, as the Health Insurance Act did not cover children. As a result, school inspection often boiled down to being a yearly inspection for head lice.

Concern for children at school also extended to children when they left school. It was felt that many school leavers went into jobs which had no career prospects of any kind and were just blind-alley occupations. In an attempt to prevent this, when Labour Exchanges were set up for adults, Juvenile Advisory Committees were attached to them. Later, special Junior Employment Bureaux were established.

Children in Trouble
Herbert Samuel, Under Secretary at the Home Office, was very much the champion of children who were in trouble or being exploited. Already there were in existence laws which aimed at protecting infant life and preventing cruelty to children. Largely through the efforts of Samuel, these were extended to cover neglect and negligence. It was also made an offence for children to beg or to smoke.

Until the twentieth century, children who broke the law were treated in the same way as adults and sent to prison. Then special Remand Homes were built where children could go while awaiting trial. Special Juvenile Courts were set up

43 This election poster of the Liberal party advertises Lloyd George's unemployment and health insurance schemes

to deal with child offenders. The emphasis was not so much on punishment, but on treatment in an effort to prevent a child from repeating an offence and possibly ending up as a hardened criminal.

These measures reflected the changing attitude of government and society towards children. They were now not regarded solely as the responsibility of their parents, but of the community generally. By 1914 the State had begun to make itself responsible for the welfare of the individual. The social reforms passed by the Liberal government were really the corner stones of future welfare services, but still it was only a beginning. Two world wars were to have a dramatic impact.

Further reading
M. Bruce, *The Coming of the Welfare State* (Batsford)
C. L. Mowat, *Lloyd George* (O.U.P.)

8 Between Two World Wars, 1919-1939

In 1918 the First World War ended. It had brought chaos and destruction to many parts of Europe. In England, many changes had taken place which radically altered the structure and organisation of society. Women over 30 years of age were given the right to vote—a triumph finally of the Suffragette Movement and also a recognition of the work women had done during the war years.

Education Act, 1918
There was a general feeling of optimism that the condition of life for most people would improve once the war was over. This was reflected by the passing of a new Education Act in 1918. Parents who had grown used to the idea of elementary schooling were anxious to extend opportunities for their children. By the new Act, the school leaving age was raised to fourteen. Local Authorities were also given permission to provide nursery schools for pre-school children and also to allow pupils to stay at school until they were fifteen. There were also schemes to provide part-time day continuation education up to 18. But the Act, although forward-looking and imaginative, was not put into practice completely, largely due to the cuts in spending the government had to make because of the economic situation.

44 By the 1930s many schools had improved. Classrooms were lighter and less formal than the old Board schools. Milk was provided free for pupils

In 1924 an important report on education appeared, the Hadow Report. It recommended that secondary education should be available for all children and that there should be a division between primary and secondary at the age of 11. The older classes in the elementary schools were to become 'modern' schools. Later a third type of school providing technical education was recommended. This provided the pattern for the educational system to be established after the Second World War. Also the free places at grammar schools were to be abolished, and replaced by 'special places'. This meant that parents would pay for their child's education according to their means, but Local Authority grants were available.

Concern was shown for children in need of care and also the young offenders. The Children and Young Persons Act, 1933 made parents responsible for their children until the age of 17. The old Remand Homes were replaced by Approved Schools which were run by the Local Education Authority and not the police. The emphasis now was on helping the child back to a normal life rather than cutting him off from society.

Problems in Peace Time

Generally the years after 1918 were most difficult. In spite of Lloyd George's promises of 'an England fit for heroes', returning soldiers found difficulty in getting jobs and houses and there seemed little prospect of any improvement. The main problem was that the old heavy industries, which had formed the basis of England's prosperity in the nineteenth century were floundering—iron and steel, shipbuilding, coalmining, railways were all in difficulties. The situation was particularly difficult in coalmining. In an effort to deal with the problem of declining profits mine owners cut miners' wages and also attempted to lengthen hours worked. Partly as a result of this the miners went on strike. The miners were joined by other big unions, the railwaymen and the Transport and General Workers Union and other unions called out by the TUC. This became a General Strike. It started on 4 May, 1926, but was over in 10 days, when other unions, not wishing to have an outright clash with troops, gave in. The miners struggled on alone for six months. Finally they were forced back to work in November, 1926 and had to accept lower wages.

Employment conditions did not improve. In the 1930s unemployment was a very desperate problem. Many factories were closed down. The situation was particularly bad in the North East of England, especially after the closing of the big shipbuilding yard at Jarrow. Once again it seemed that poverty, unemployment, lack of housing—the spectres of the nineteenth century—were very much apparent.

The Poor Law Reorganised

Nevertheless in spite of economic difficulties, some important changes were made which furthered the development of the Welfare State. In 1929 the Local

45 Poverty was still an acute problem in the inter-war years. Here food is being distributed to poor people in Shoreditch, London

Government Act reorganised the Poor Law. It was very much needed as so many different services had developed since the nineteenth century that there was a lot of overlapping. For example, Local Authorities might find themselves short of hospitals, yet a Poor Law Infirmary might be standing half-empty. As a result of the new Act, many small authorities disappeared and the Poor Law Guardians were finally abolished. When the name Poor Law disappeared in 1929, the whole service was renamed Public Assistance and was to be concerned with old people, sick people, widows and orphans. The unemployed, however, still faced a problem. If they were receiving National Insurance 'benefit' then they were dealt with by the Ministry of Labour; if not, then they came under the Poor Law—later, Public Assistance.

Unemployment

A special scheme was drawn up in an attempt to deal with the unemployment problem, which, as we have seen, was particularly acute in the 1930s. Originally it had been confidently expected that the National Insurance Act would have been enough. But never, at any time, had it been expected that people would actually live on benefit. In 1911 this had been 7s (35p) a week, and although the amount had more than doubled by the 1930s, even this did not cover the rise in the cost of living. In 1931 a system of allowances was established. These existed side-by-side with insurance contributions and were based on need. Once a man's benefit from insurance had run out and he still had no job, then he would apply for benefit from the Unemployment Assistance Board.

The Unemployment Assistance Board lasted until 1948—although its name was changed in 1940 to the Assistance Board. The rate given was 24s (£1.20) for a man and wife with allowances for children. There was also a small allowance for rent. But unemployment assistance was not given automatically; a man had to prove his poverty and need by undergoing a Means Test. This was based on the income of a whole household, and included money of children who were earning. It caused a lot of family strife, particularly where a wife was supporting her

46 Because of unemployment during the 1930s many men were forced to register at Labour Exchanges such as this one in Birmingham

husband or grown up children, their parents and the rest of the family. The Means Test was hated. The only advantage it had was that information about family income was taken by a visiting official: at least families did not have to declare their poverty before a whole Poor Law Committee.

Social Investigations

During the 1930s the whole question of poverty was attracting attention. Even those who were working were often still very poor as their wages were so low. There were complaints then, as there are today, that those on assistance were 'better off' than those at work. In the 1930s it was in fact the case that families were often better off when the father was unemployed as they did then at least receive extra payments for dependants. A survey made in Bristol in 1938 showed that in one-third of the city's poorest families the father was employed and received no help from the social services. It was this kind of situation that caused Eleanor Rathbone to campaign so vigorously for Family Allowances for everyone, although these were not introduced until after the Second World War.

Another investigation into poverty in York was made by Seebohm Rowntree. What he revealed was shattering. About one-fifth of the working class were living below a poverty line which was itself very spartan. The York and Bristol surveys revealed that about one-third of working-class children were inadequately fed. This was not just happening in slum areas, but also in new housing estates where extreme poverty was often caused because the rents were so high.

Housing

Housing generally was still an acute problem in this inter-war period. We have already seen that Local Authorities had been given power by an Act of 1890 to build houses, but had not made much use of it. Private builders had built blocks of flats in many cities in the last quarter of the nineteenth century, but the cost of land and building materials in the twentieth century made it impossible for them to go on doing this. The only remedy was for the government to give financial

47 In the North East unemployment was particularly high after the closure of the shipyard at Jarrow. From here the men started the famous hunger march to London in 1936

aid to Local Authorities to build houses. During the 1920s, as a result of government subsidies, Local Authority estates were built up and down the country. They were very ugly, quite unimaginative, but certainly better than the slum horrors they often replaced.

During the 1930s vigorous efforts were made at slum clearance. The aim was not just to pull down slums, but to rehouse the people living in them. A five-year limit was set and a quarter of a million homes were to be pulled down. In fact by 1939 only half had been cleared. It was not until the Second World War, when many slum residents were evacuated, that the public conscience was really roused. As in other areas, plans were made to do something once the war was over.

So, during the period between the wars the development of welfare services was slow. Various schemes for improving the quality of life through housing and education started in the 1920s, but did not come to very much. This was due to economic problems—a general shortage of money to pay for such schemes. The 1930s were marred by the spectre of unemployment and the growing threat of war. The war years themselves, 1939–1945, were not entirely unprofitable. During them a lot of hard thinking was done and a government blueprint for social reform—new measures concerning health, unemployment, insurance, education and town planning—was drawn up.

Further reading
P. Lane, *Documents on British Economic and Social History 1870–1939* (Macmillan)
G. Orwell, *The Road to Wigan Pier* (Penguin)
Seebohm Rowntree, *Poverty and Progress* (Longmans)

48 (*opposite*) Slums still existed in the 1930s: Queen Ann Street, Liverpool

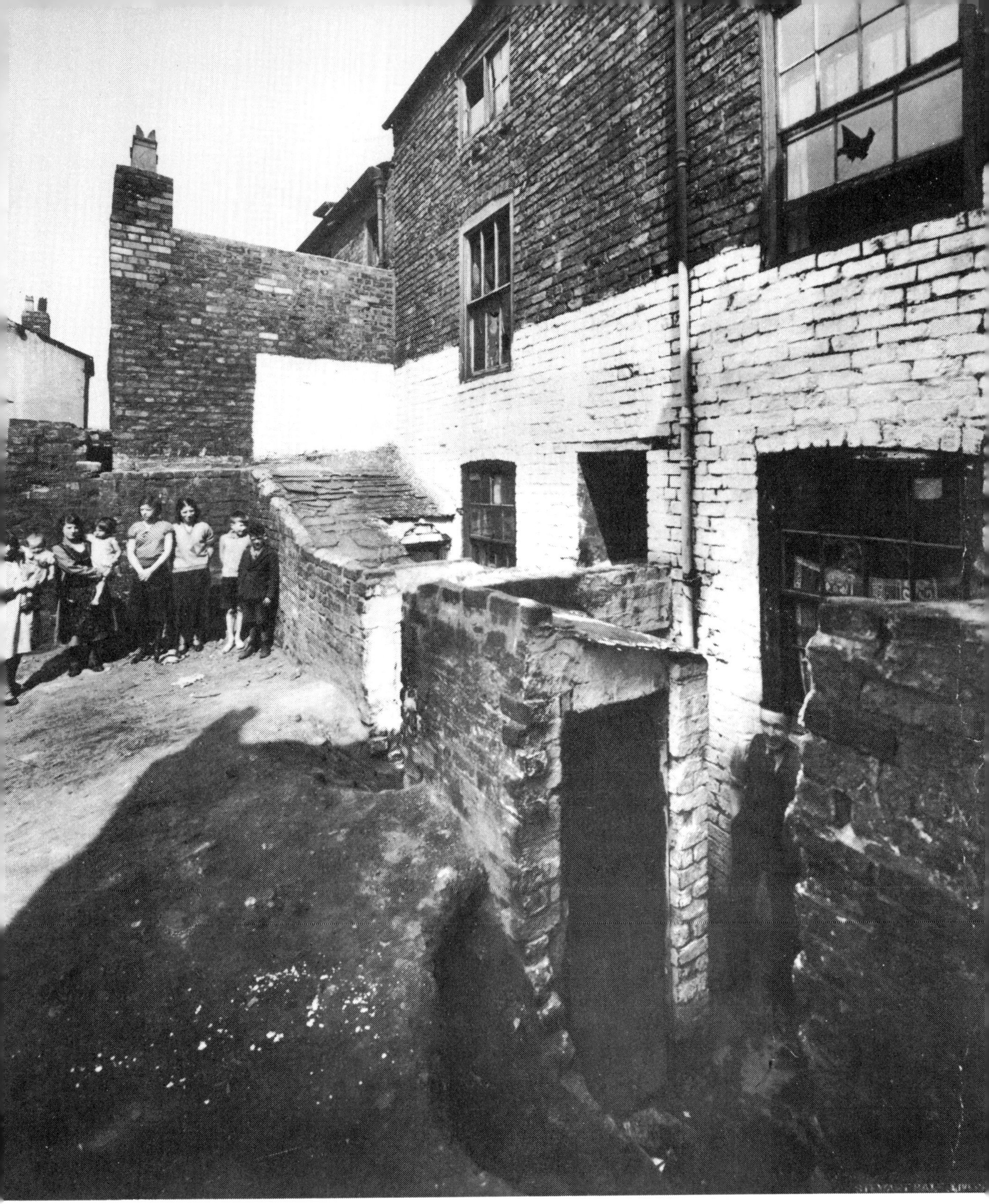

9 Welfare from 1939

The Impact of War

In 1939 the Second World War against Germany started. Already the government had plans prepared to cope with the fighting forces, the production of armaments and the general direction of the war effort. Also, during the war years 1939–1945 the State played a much more direct part in peoples lives by organising work and welfare. This government intervention during the war years is sometimes referred to as 'war socialism'.

The operation of 'war socialism' was carried out much more efficiently during the Second World War than the First World War, when everything tended to be done on the spur of the moment as each crisis arose. Different groups of people—such as the civil servants, businessmen and university teachers—had then learned to co-ordinate their efforts to cope with the administration and strategy of the war. By the time the Second World War began, their previous experience had enabled them to lay plans, and they already had experience of working together. By 1939 another group, the Trade Union officials, had joined this team. The emphasis was now on co-operating to win the war and a common outlook was much more important than social background.

Those running the war had many problems to cope with on the home front—the effects of air raids, the distribution of food supplies and war equipment. The railways had to bear a particularly heavy burden. Channel ports and those on the East Coast were closed during the war years. This meant that coal from the North East had to be taken by rail to the South, and cargoes of frozen meat and steel had to be distributed by rail. Also, during the war years, the number of passengers using the railways increased due to scarcity of petrol for private motor cars and a general feeling that travel by rail was safer. Another complication was that the railways were still in private hands. But, largely due to the efforts of the Ministry of Supply, arrangements were made for freight wagons to be pooled. Trains would run over lines belonging to rival companies. In effect, during the war years the government organised and controlled the railways. Thus it was only a short step to nationalisation in 1947. The government also organised ports so that transport and shipping could be linked together more closely. Port Directors were appointed and they arranged the distribution of imports.

The war also meant closer government control of industry. Aeroplanes had to be produced and fighting equipment for the army, navy and air force. The government also had to keep the people at home happy and cheerful. The Board of Trade largely controlled what factories produced. Some factories continued to work full time, others were used for storage. As so much was needed for the war effort a limit had to be placed on the manufacture of other goods. 'Utility' furniture was devised, which was very functional. It came up to specified standards, but was not in any way luxurious. The Board of Trade also introduced the 'rationing' of clothes. Obviously not so many clothes could be made during the war years, so what was available was shared out. 'Rationing' was later extended to food. The Ministry of Food based the rationing on a scientifically planned nutritive diet. This was not very appetising, but on the whole, the British people were better fed during the war than before it.

To save importing corn, the Ministry of Agriculture encouraged crop growing by farmers rather than dairy farming. Between 1939 and 1941 nearly four million acres were ploughed up. It was estimated that this saved about twenty-two million tons of shipping used for imports, and this could then be used for the war effort.

As a result of so much government intervention and regulation of economic life there was no really acute shortage of food or war materials. The supply of

49 Bomb damage was very extensive. Whole areas such as this in Swansea had to be cleared and houses rebuilt

50 Rationing of food and clothing remained in force for many years after the war

labour, however, was another problem. The army was constantly needing men, but men were also needed at home in the factories which were producing fighting equipment. The dilemma was partially solved by the recruitment of women for the army and the allocation of men to the most vital industries. In many ways the war helped the class struggle in England. Everyone felt they were fighting for a common cause and workers were not so conscious of being exploited by 'the boss'.

In 1945 the Second World War ended. During the years that followed the foundations of the Welfare State were consolidated. The post-war problems that faced the government were immense. Forty thousand people had died during the war, four million homes had been destroyed by bomb damage. Food and clothing had been shared out during the war years by means of rationing. Rationing and ration books remained in force for several years after 1945.

To cope with such problems, the social services had been extended and adapted during the war years. Supplementary pensions had been introduced in 1940. The hated household Means Test had been abolished in 1941. A national milk scheme for all mothers and young children was established. Cod liver oil and vitamin tablets were available free to them. School meals were extended and subsidised. Immunisation against certain illnesses—scarlet fever, diphtheria, whooping cough, smallpox etc.—was much more common. The nation as a whole was becoming increasingly health-conscious.

William Beveridge

Already a blue-print for future welfare services was in existence. William Beveridge had drawn up his *Report* in 1942 for the government. He used statistics from investigations of Seebohm Rowntree and others. Beveridge showed that on the basis of pre-war conditions it should be possible to abolish want merely by redistributing the income of wage earners. He wanted the State to play a much more positive rôle by providing a wider and more comprehensive health service, insurance schemes against mass unemployment, allowances for families, pensions for retirement—not just old age. Beveridge's scheme was not adopted entirely but it did stamp out a pattern for future developments.

Family Allowances

Before the war had ended the Coalition government had set up a Ministry of National Insurance and passed a Family Allowances Act. When the Labour government was elected in 1945 they announced that Family Allowances would be paid by 5 August, 1946. These allowances were for all families. They did not depend on any contribution. Each family was allowed 5s (25p) for each child after the first. Today Family Allowances are still paid, but the allowance is taxable. This means that better-off families, who do not really need an allowance from the State for their children, pay it back in the form of income tax. The introduction of Family Allowances was an important step forward. Largely because of the

51   William Beveridge (1899–1963) was largely responsible for the form of development the social services took after the Second World War. Hospitals, some of which, like St Bartholomew's in London, had been developed from medieval monastic foundations, now operated as part of the National Health Service

vigorous campaigning of Eleanor Rathbone the allowance was made payable to the mother—a recognition of the rights of the housewife and the importance of the family in society. Also the introduction of Family Allowances showed the positive result of the work of Rowntree and others whose investigations had revealed that even when a father was in work the wage might be so low that it would not support a family.

National Insurance
The introduction of a comprehensive National Insurance scheme was the culmination of a long campaign dating from the end of the nineteenth century. A start had been made, as we have seen, in 1911 but it needed extending. What was laid down in the new scheme largely exists today—only the amount of the insurance stamp has changed. Every working person paid an insurance stamp to cover unemployment, pension, health and injury at work. Of course the individual contribution did not cover the cost of all that had to be provided so the rest had to come from income tax. In 1966 there was a new National Insurance Bill which suggested that benefits for unemployment and sickness should be related to what one earned. The issue, which is still not resolved, is that in making equal payments to everyone it happens that benefit is paid to the wealthy who do not need it. What did come about in 1966 was an administrative change. The Ministry of National Insurance was replaced by the Ministry of Social Security. Today insurance and health both come under the Department of Health and Social Security.

Pensions
In principle the insurance scheme should provide for all. But there still remain the old, mentally sick and disabled who cannot work, cannot pay their stamp and must be provided for. Pensions for old age had already been introduced in 1909. Gradually the amount had increased. It is paid to men reaching the age of 65 and women at 60. In 1965 it was £5 a week. In 1971 it was nearly £9 for a married couple and increases continue. Even so, the cost of living has risen very dramatically. A pension only provides a very meagre standard of living, particularly for those who have no savings to draw on. Again there is the anomaly that a State pension is paid to everyone and certainly goes to some who are wealthy enough not to need it. But if savings had the effect of reducing pensions this too would seem unfair. Those who have only their pension to live on can apply for extra—called supplementary benefit—which is only paid to people who have little or no savings.

National Assistance Board
In 1948 the National Assistance Board was set up to provide help for those who could not work. These included people who stayed at home looking after elderly parents, unmarried mothers, deserted or separated mothers with young children. But the Board suffered from the disadvantage of being associated with Public

52 Training the unemployed for new work was an essential part of the work of the Ministry of Labour. Here workers are being retrained at a centre in Wales

Assistance and the pre-war Means Test. In 1966 this problem was partially overcome as the Assistance Board was merged with the Ministry of Social Security. The amounts paid out are minimal and near-poverty is still an added burden to those suffering from disablement or distressed circumstances.

Children

The plight of many children had become painfully noticeable during the war years when many were evacuated from city areas to the countryside. Often these children were underfed, undernourished, and undereducated. Already, by the end of the war, measures had been taken to extend school milk and meals.

It was recognised, too, that orphaned children and those from broken homes were especially at risk. In 1948 the Children's Act made each Local Authority responsible for providing a home for children whose parents could not look after them. Many children's homes run by voluntary societies already existed. Other measures helped to improve conditions for children and to preserve the unity of the family. For example, day nurseries were provided so working mothers had somewhere to put their babies when they went out to work; holidays were arranged for mothers with young children; reception centres were set up for mothers and children who were, for various reasons, temporarily homeless. Local Authorities also had the task of making sure that houses were fit to live in and that there was no overcrowding.

Although this list sounds impressive, in practice the services actually provided were not very efficient. The main drawback was that there were so many separate authorities responsible for different things. As a result there was often confusion and overlapping. This was felt by many voluntary societies who worked outside the Local Authority. These tried to deal with each family as a unit instead of sending separate social workers to the same family to deal with various problems.

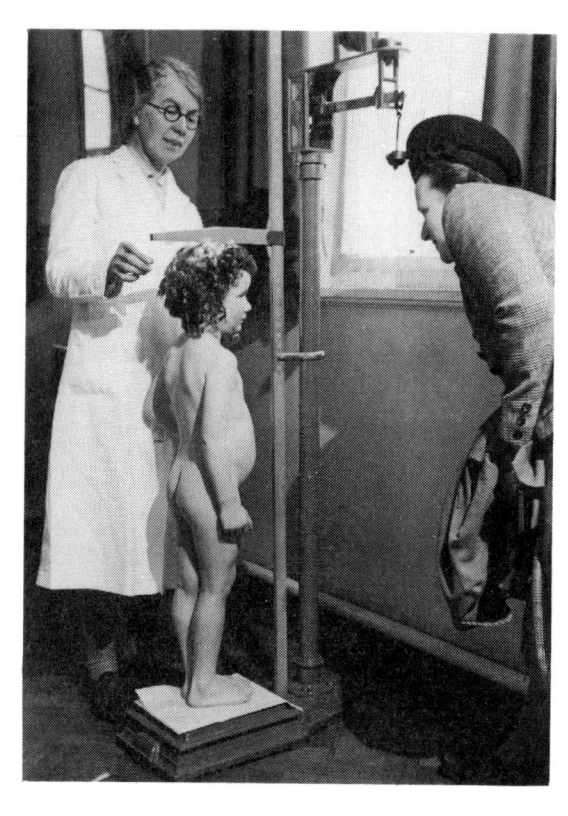

53 It was found by nutrition experts that children's health had improved during the war years

The valuable work done by the voluntary societies was recognised by the Children and Young Persons Act, 1963 which allowed Local Authorities to work directly with the voluntary societies. Local Authorities were also encouraged to give direct help to families in need—for example, payment of rent arrears, travelling expenses to visit a sick member of the family in hospital, and grants for school uniform. The importance of preserving the family unit was emphasised by the Seebohm Report (1968). This pointed out what the voluntary societies had already recognised—that families who have one problem often have several. It emphasised the distress caused to individual families by visits from different social workers. The report recommended that one social worker should be attached to a family and deal with all that family's problems regarding housing, children, finance or whatever arose.

Further reading
M. Bruce, *The Coming of the Welfare State* (Batsford)
P. Gregg, *The Welfare State* (Harrap)
P. Lane, *Documents on British Economic and Social History 1945–1967* (Macmillan)
E. N. and A. M. Newth, *Britain in the Modern World: The Twentieth Century* (Penguin)
Lady Williams, *The Coming of the Welfare State* (G. Allen & Unwin)

10 Education, 1944-1970

The Second World War had also shown gaps in the educational system. The educational standards of children evacuated had caused a great deal of concern and interest. Also the lack of any really efficient technical education was evident during the war years. As a result, even before the war ended, a new Education Act was passed.

1944 Education Act

The aim of this Act was to provide a complete education for all. Each Local Authority was to see that children were educated according to their individual 'age, ability and aptitude'. Parents had the legal responsibility of seeing that their children were properly educated. The new Act was really based on ideas and recommendations that had appeared in important educational reports during the inter-war period. Education was to be provided in three stages—primary, secondary and further education. Local Authorities were also encouraged to provide nursery schools for younger children. The school leaving age was raised from fourteen to fifteen. In fact, it was suggested in 1944, that it should be raised to sixteen as soon as it was practicable to do so although this did not materialise until the date was set for 1973.

The 1944 Act showed that the old idea of elementary education going right through to fourteen or fifteen years was disappearing. The idea of secondary education for all seemed to be approaching. But there were no actual directions given in the Act as to the form secondary education should take. In fact, suggestions were adopted that had been made in earlier reports on education which led towards a system of secondary, technical, and secondary modern schools. A special committee which met in 1943 recommended an exam for all children in State schools at eleven.

The three types of school were all supposed to have the same prestige level. This did not work out in practice as grammar schools came to be more favoured by parents. The 'eleven plus' exam came to be seen in terms of pass or fail which caused a lot of unnecessary distress to children and parents alike.

Comprehensive Schools

The idea of abolishing the eleven plus exam and establishing large neighbourhood schools for all children has developed considerably. In fact in some areas, such as the Isle of Man, comprehensive schools were established before the end of the Second World War. By 1957 there were 61 comprehensive schools; by 1965, 289. Eighty of these were in London. By 1968 the total number had risen to 748.

54 A new purpose-built comprehensive school

The idea of a comprehensive school became very much entangled with politics. The Labour government in 1966 committed itself to providing comprehensive schools. When Labour lost the general election in 1970 a lot of comprehensive schemes were halted by the new Conservative Minister of Education, Margaret Thatcher.

There are several arguments in favour of comprehensive schools. Under the old system of selection at eleven, many children regarded themselves as failures if they did not gain a grammar school place. Often children's potential development could not be forecast at eleven with any degree of accuracy so there was likely to be wastage of talent. It was felt too that with all children attending the same school, class and intellectual divisions could be done away with. There are also important educational arguments. With no eleven plus the junior school has more freedom to plan the work it wants to do. The comprehensive school, being large, can provide a wide variety of courses, more attractive buildings—if built especially as a comprehensive—and facilities.

55 The University of Sussex

Primary Schools

There have also been important developments, since the 1944 Act, in primary education. In 1963, the Conservative Minister for Education, Sir Edward Boyle, set up a special committee to look into primary schools. Altogether twenty thousand schools were investigated. The final report, named after the Chairman, Lady Plowden, was published in 1967. The report emphasised the important connexion between a child's home background and its performance at school. It showed too that a child learnt more by finding things out for himself rather than just being told by the teacher. It stressed the rôle of the school within the community. The report particularly revealed that slum buildings were still being used for many primary schools in inner city areas. It was found that overcrowding, inefficient heating systems and outside lavatories were quite common.

Partly as a result of the *Plowden Report*, special schemes were introduced into certain areas with particular problems. These are known as Educational Priority Areas. Many of the school buildings are old, but to compensate for this, it was recommended that the average number of children in each class should be smaller, and more money allocated to these schools for equipment and school visits. In 1971 the Conservative government announced that it would be spending a considerable amount of money on improving primary schools.

Further and Higher Education

The need for technical education had been seen during the Second World War, when it was felt that technicians and engineers were particularly scarce. Local Authorities were encouraged to have their own technical colleges. In the 1960s university education was also extended. New universities such as Sussex and Kent were built and older universities were enlarged. Larger technical colleges became polytechnics and some can now award their own degrees. Teacher Training Colleges had their name changed to Colleges of Education and the length of teacher training was extended from two years to three; and later with a fourth year available to some students who wished to qualify for a degree in education. Most of these developments in the field of higher education came about as a result of the Robbins Report—a special committee that was set up in 1961 to investigate higher education.

Another exciting development has been the Open University, which began its courses in January 1971. Students of this university work on their own at home and are taught by means of special programmes on the radio and television. They are older students who possibly missed the opportunity of higher education when they were younger. Most of them have jobs and do their studying in their spare time.

Further reading
Children and their Primary Schools (1967, HMSO)
R. Pedley, *The Comprehensive School* (Penguin)

11 Health and Housing from 1945

The National Health Service, 1948

As we have seen there had been much concern over the nation's health since the beginning of the twentieth century. Already a start towards a Health Service had been made in 1911, but it needed two world wars before a full, comprehensive service could be established. Enormous advances had been made in the discovery of new drugs, while nursing and medical skills had improved. But the Second World War had created new problems—mutilation from bomb damage, the possible escalation of developing weapons with the attendant threat of future radiation—whilst on a more immediate level the war had created a shortage of men and materials.

During the war the Health Service had been extended. The yearly income limit which established who could take part in the scheme had been raised to £420 per year. But this still meant that only about half the population could participate. There were also other gaps. The old Health Service did not provide specialist treatment in hospital, nor did it provide dental treatment, spectacles or hearing aids. Mental illness was not included. Even the spread of doctors around the country as a whole was uneven. Large, industrial cities such as Liverpool and Manchester had few doctors in proportion to the population whereas wealthy seaside resorts on the South Coast had almost too many.

The organisation of the hospital service was also very haphazard. Many hospitals had originally been founded by private individuals or voluntary societies. In 1945, there were about one thousand of these. Some were excellently run and well equipped; others were just small, local cottage hospitals. Besides the voluntary hospitals Local Authorities had their own hospitals. Some of these had been set up especially, others had developed from the sick wards of the old workhouses. On the whole, most were not well equipped either with staff or resources.

Besides the hospital service there were other medical services. Each Local Authority had its own Medical Officer of Health. There were also special Medical Inspectors for factories to see that health standards were maintained there, and Sanitary Inspectors who looked after cleansing of towns, sewage disposal and anything likely to damage the health of an area. Local Authorities also provided a medical service for schools. There were special maternity and child care services, also special treatment clinics for tuberculosis.

So one can see that with all these various divisions there was a great need for reorganisation. Beveridge had already laid down plans for the creation of a general health service in his Report of 1942. In 1945, Aneurin Bevan, the Labour Minister of Health, intended to put most of Beveridge's plans into practice. Bevan

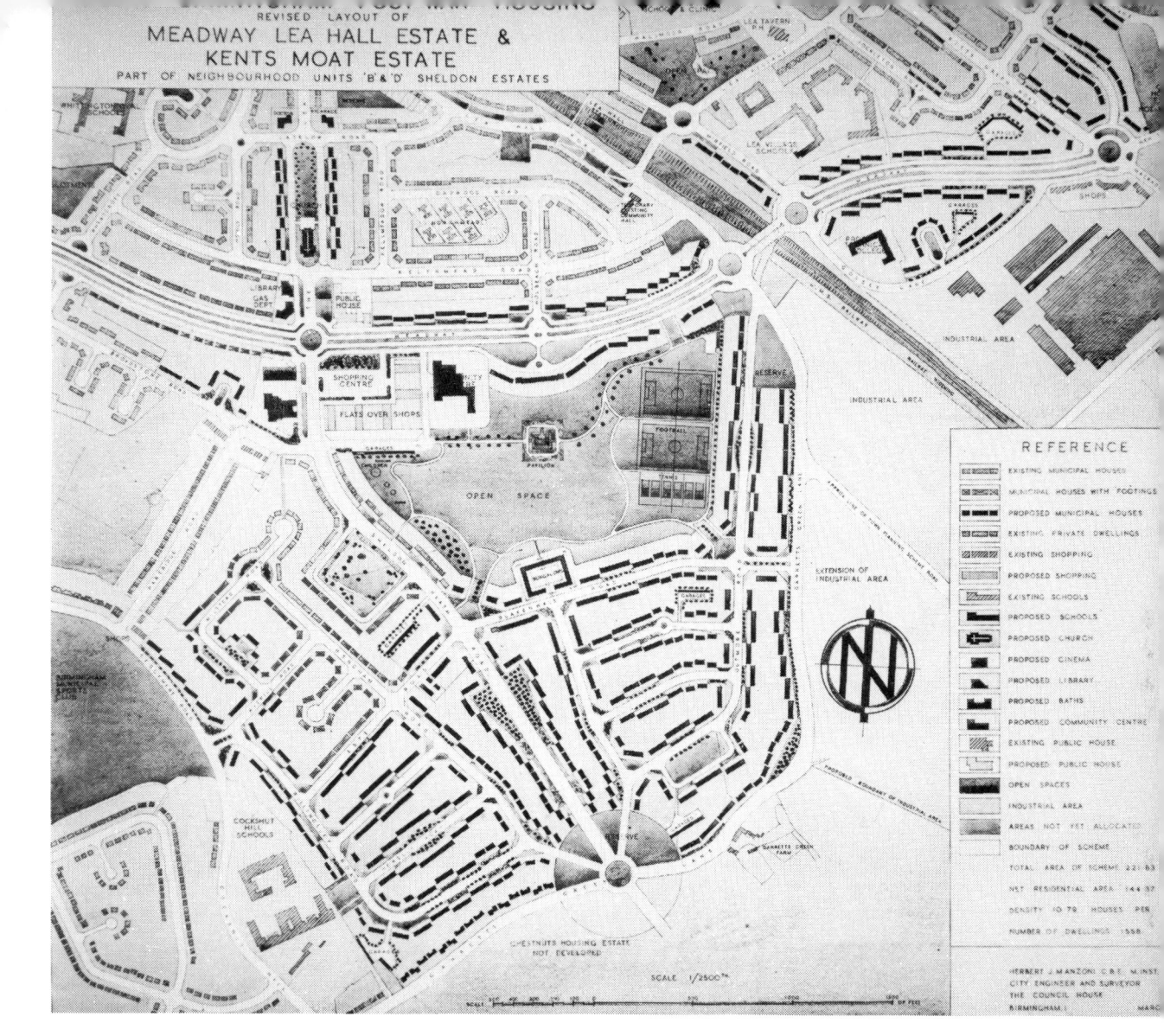

56 Many post-war housing schemes hoped to provide for a whole new community and included plans not only for houses but also for factories, schools, shops and leisure facilities

agreed with Beveridge's basic principle that the State's first duty was the 'restoration of a sick person to health'. It took Bevan three years to put these plans into operation. It involved him in bitter disputes with the medical profession and lengthy negotiations with Local Authorities.

Bevan was determined that there should be no income limit for the new Health Service as this would result in a 'two tier' system: in reality, one for the rich who could pay and one for the poor, who would have to accept whatever was going. Bevan intended to include everyone. He realised that insurance alone would not cover the cost of a Health Service. The extra would have to come from taxation.

73

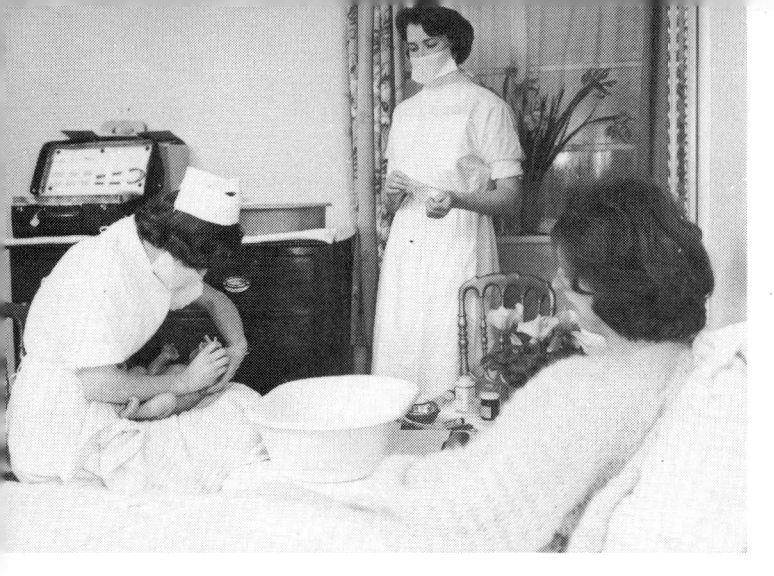

57 As the Health Service developed, maternity and midwifery services improved. Here a domicilary midwife supervises a pupil midwife while the mother looks on

In other words the rich would, in fact, pay more towards the Health Service as they paid more in tax. Everyone, however, would make the same weekly contribution by means of an insurance stamp.

Bevan intended that the new Health Service should be run by the Ministry of Health. It would be run in sections. Provision made by Local Authorities would be the preventative services. These would include vaccination and immunisation, health visitors and home nurses, maternity services, midwives and ambulances. Local Authorities were also to be responsible for environmental services—that is making sure that the locality was fit to live in. This included responsibility for street cleansing, water supply, and the prevention of nuisances.

The hospital service was reorganised. The hospitals were divided into Regional Hospital Groups. Each region was to have its own board and medical school. Some of the voluntary hospitals had to close down because of lack of money; others opted to join a Regional Hospital Group. Negotiations with the medical profession were very lengthy. Eventually a compromise was reached that patients could opt out of the Health Service and have private treatment from their doctor or hospital specialist if they wished.

Finally, in 1948, Lloyd George's Health Insurance scheme came to an end. A free medical service for all was now provided under the Ministry of Health. Certainly the public responded enthusiastically. Three-quarters of the population registered with the National Health Service. It was a great achievement for Labour politicians. Bevan himself called it 'the most civilised achievement of modern government'. In 1960 Harold Wilson referred to the National Health Service as 'the very temple of our social security system' but the National Health Service has come under much criticism in the 1960s and 1970s. Political battles over whether charges for prescriptions should be made have been fought. At first it was intended that everything should be free, but prohibitive costs of certain drugs that are prescribed with frequency—penicillin, antibiotics, tranquillisers, barbiturates—have caused that decision to be reversed. Under the Conservative government in 1971 a charge of 20p was made for each item on a prescription.

58 The School Medical Service has grown with the Health Service. Many large comprehensive schools have their own Medical Suite where routine examinations can take place

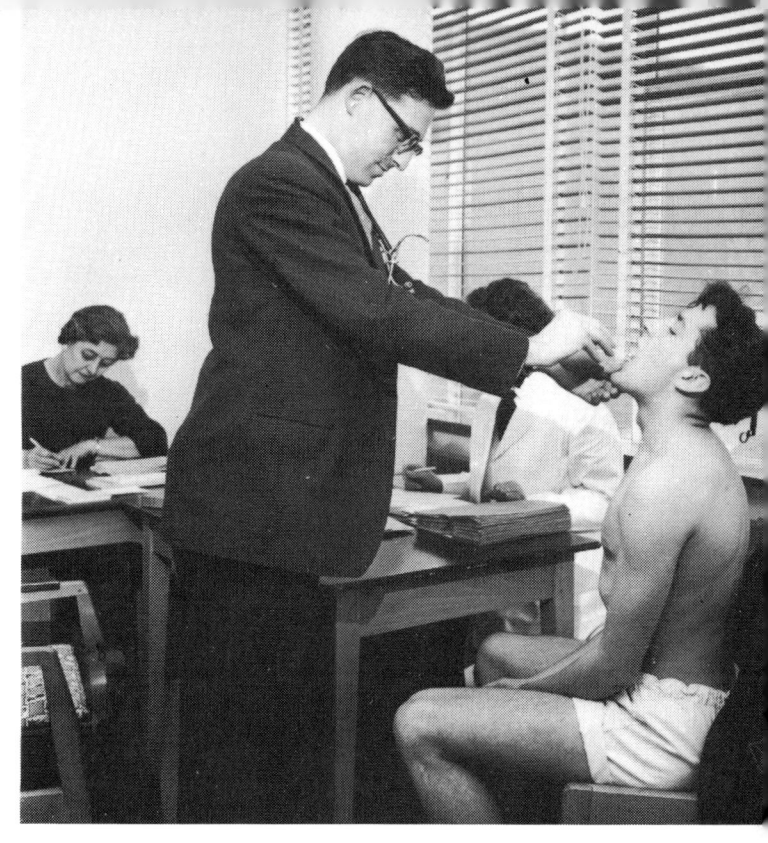

Chronic sufferers can still get their drugs free, but this is not automatic and requires forms filled in by the applicant and endorsed by the doctor and chemist.

The Health Service is a very important feature of the Welfare State. It also provokes a lot of controversy. Many people resent paying towards a Health Service they do not themselves use. Some resent foreigners and temporary visitors receiving free medical treatment in England. Controversy also rages over issues that come within the fringe of the Health Service in certain circumstances, such as abortion, sterilisation and treatment for drug addicts. But whatever the criticisms, the Health Service does provide medical help for all who need it. The main problem, at present, is the continued financing of the service.

Housing

Another acute post-war problem was housing. Bombs had damaged millions of homes during the war. Almost overnight in 1945 'squatters' had appeared in luxury flats in the West End and refused to move. Some speedy remedy had to be found. A temporary answer was 'prefabs' which were run up rapidly and provided 92,000 homes in eighteen months.

But the housing problem generally was to remain and still no real solution has been found. Aggravating the post-war housing problem was the fact that people were marrying earlier and were wanting larger families. Also with the war over there was a demand for goods which had been unavailable during war time. Obviously these had to be put somewhere.

One advance had taken place. New building methods had been discovered which meant that high-rise flats could be built quickly. In fact many of these blocks were put up so quickly that the long term problems of dull architecture and the isolation of families living there were not considered. But even the speed of high-rise flat building could not keep pace with population growth. By 1965 more than three million families in Great Britain were living in slums.

There were also other problems to be considered. How many houses should be built by Local Authorities? How many by private builders? Should more houses be available to rent or to buy? There was also the problem that some tenants were paying rent that was very low as it had been controlled since the First World War. This meant that the landlord could not increase it. In 1959 the Conservative government passed a Rent Act which removed rent control from about 800,000 houses. This was done in the belief that it would encourage more people to let their houses and flats and that it would also encourage landlords to carry out repairs. This did not happen. There was no spectacular rise in the number of houses or flats available for letting. In fact by the mid 1960s there was even more overcrowding as flats were increasingly subdivided.

Rent Act 1965

Rent control was reintroduced in 1965 by the new Labour government. This was largely as a result of the findings of a housing report on Greater London. This report revealed gross ill-treatment of tenants and chronic overcrowding. In fact many of the photographs were painfully reminiscent of the nineteenth-century slum rather than life in the twentieth century.

The new Act gave security of tenure. This was a form of guarantee that you could remain in possession of your house or flat for a specified period and could not be evicted. Rents were also frozen at their existing level. This meant that landlords could not put rent up. The new Act applied to property of up to £400 per annum rateable value in London, and £200 elsewhere. It was made a crime to evict tenants without a court order, or to harass or intimidate them. The Act applied to furnished and unfurnished accommodation and it did give some protection to tenants, but it did not solve the basic problem of there being insufficient housing. Local Authorities are building more houses to rent, but with rising building costs the rent is high and beyond the reach of the poorer section of the population. In 1971 the Conservative government removed rent control.

59 New housing at Park Hill, Sheffield, Yorkshire. The nineteenth-century school (left) still remains

60 A New Town: Cumbernauld near Glasgow. In the foreground is Cumbernauld High School. This aerial view shows the interesting layout of the housing areas

'Shelter'

The problem of homelessness has not been dealt with satisfactorily by any government. As with other areas within the Welfare State, voluntary help does what it can. 'Shelter', an organisation for helping the homeless, was founded in 1967. It has special experimental branches, for example the Shelter Housing Aid Centre which offers help to London families in buying a house and getting a mortgage. Shelter Neighbourhood Action Group has concentrated on a twilight area in Liverpool, bought up and converted homes and made them habitable. Shelter has done a lot to emphasise the plight of many people who are forced to live in squalid conditions as late as the 1970s. In a report published in 1971, Shelter has revealed that for many people the nineteenth-century slum is very much a reality.

Further reading
P. Gregg, *The Welfare State* (Harrap)
S. Healy, *Town Life* (Batsford)
N. Longmate, *Alive and Well* (Penguin)

12 The Welfare State Today

Throughout the 1950s it was generally believed that poverty in Britain had been abolished—that people were no longer poor. On the surface this was a very plausible assertion. Wages had risen considerably since the ending of the Second World War in 1945. More people had jobs. Children, on the whole, were healthier and better educated than their parents. More people could afford to buy luxury goods on hire purchase. The number of cars, radios, television sets, fridges and washing machines increased. In fact the phrase 'the affluent society' was often used to describe the 1950s in Britain.

Seebohm Rowntree made another study of poverty in York. He found that in 1950 only $1\frac{1}{2}$ per cent of the Survey population lived in poverty. In 1936 it had been 18 per cent. The hunger marches of the 1930s had faded in people's memories. Rowntree argued that the coming of the Welfare State had helped to create this new prosperity. He felt that poverty was now really confined to old age and 'problem families' who were unable to cope with their weekly budget properly. In fact Rowntree's list of what he considered 'necessities' was unrealistic and not in any way related to working-class spending habits. For example, he thought that the average working-class income should be enough to provide cheap food from which sufficient nutrition would be obtained. He did not take into account, however, that the over-worked mothers, with little time and inadequate cooking facilities, could not often undertake the necessary preparation of such food.

The complacency of the 1950s was certainly shattered in the 1960s. Attention was drawn to large sections of the population who were still finding it difficult to make both ends meet: widows, separated or single mothers, the sick and disabled, old people, in fact anyone who was unable to work and had to exist on fixed pensions or allowances which failed to keep pace with the rising cost of living.

Another large group were families with low incomes. A survey made by a social worker in the East End of London showed that many people there were in real need. For them the actual procedure of getting help from Social Security offices was so complicated that they gave up.

In fact the Welfare State has not abolished poverty and need. It has not, as Beveridge hoped, redistributed income. It has not yet solved the problem facing families where the father or mother works, but where the weekly income is often too low to cope with the provision of nutritious food, rent, furniture, clothing. In 1971 this problem was emphasised in a report published by the Child Poverty Action Group which showed how families were trying hard to manage on low incomes while prices were rising.

What the Welfare State does provide is some kind of safety net for the old, sick, children and unemployed. Also its rôle is changing as the needs of society and the economy—how people live and earn their living—become more complex. In fact as the State now regulates many aspects of economic life it is also becoming increasingly important in the social sphere. The State or government now controls many major industries: transport, coal, gas, electricity, steel, sections of the mass media (certain radio and television channels). Exports and imports of goods coming into the country and leaving it are also strictly controlled. Everyone now needs a passport to enter and leave the country. Immigration to Britain is limited, the government also interferes in other aspects of economic life. It has a considerable influence on Trade Unions and settlement of wage claims.

In the field of welfare the State also plays a much wider, if sometimes ineffective rôle. We can see problems which were present in the nineteenth century still unresolved in the twentieth. Tensions—practical and psychological—which arise from the pressure of living and working in crowded towns are there. Advances in technology creating redundancies and unemployment and enforced leisure is another problem. The foundations of the Welfare State laid in 1945 have needed massive expansion and are still barely adequate.

Education

The inadequacy of original provisions is illustrated by education. Compulsory schooling from five to fifteen, eventually sixteen years has meant the massive building of new schools and the improvement of old ones to cope with the expanding population. As a result of research into the needs of pre-school children there is a growing demand for nursery schools. Some Local Authorities do provide these, but most nursery schools are to be found largely in middle-class areas. The needs of the young pre-school child in inner urban areas are still not being met.

61 Unemployment is still a problem in the 1950s. A slump in the car industry in 1957 caused many people to lose their jobs

62 Housing in the 1970s: a new development at Thetford

Playgroups also exist in many parts of the country, but many of these are run on a shoestring and often on a voluntary basis.

In secondary schools, as in primary, more money for books, equipment, audio-visual aids is needed. With the raising of the school leaving age to sixteen, the needs of the adolescent must be thought out very carefully if boredom and potential violence is not to result. But many more children are opting voluntarily to stay on at school and want further specialist education at Colleges of Further Education, Polytechnics, University etc. This has resulted in an increase in the amount spent on grants to students. The needs of students—now adults at eighteen with the right to vote—need to be considered. The attempt by the Minister of Education, Mrs Thatcher, to control Student Union funds has proved most unpopular. Students, whether at school, University or any sector of higher education, are demanding more influence on the way in which these institutions are run. They want their courses to be less narrowly academic and have some relevance either to the real needs of research or the society in which they will later have to find jobs.

Students, like sectors of the working class, are often very poor. They do not, however, get much sympathy as their poverty is seen as being temporary. But, in fact, even many graduates have found difficulty in obtaining the jobs they want in the early 1970s. Many female arts graduates have been forced to take jobs which they could just as well have started at sixteen or eighteen years. Often this is a result of prejudice on the part of male management in industry. Also the way in which the students' grant is allocated means that many of them, although legally adult, have to live off their parents. Often students are forced to compete with the poorer section of the working class for accommodation in large cities, thus putting poor families at an even greater disadvantage. Another problem is that some students wish to marry before they have completed their courses. For a male student this usually means an increase in his grant, but for a female a decrease.

Extension of Health and Environmental Services
As the result of the provision of a basic Health Service, more babies survive infancy and adults tend to live longer. These factors alone have resulted in many extensions to the Health Service as it was established in 1948. Maternity facilities and child welfare centres have increased. A mother usually has the choice of having her baby at home or in hospital. Welfare foods are available—orange juice, cod liver oil, vitamin tablets. But these are not provided free. People pay according to the amount they earn. Special centres too are provided for handicapped children. Earlier in the century many physically handicapped children died in early infancy. Now their needs as children and adults have to be catered for. Sometimes special schools or homes are provided for them by Local Authorities, but there are not enough places to go round. Many families have to cope, often unaided, with a physically handicapped or maladjusted child. This often has disastrous effects on the other members of the family. Equally tragic is the sight of mentally sick children who are the permanent residents in many hospitals, often having few visitors or contacts with the 'normal' world.

For the physically and mentally handicapped, whether child or adult, the Welfare State still has much to provide. Voluntary societies, private charities do their best raising money by such means as holding flag days and sponsored charity walks. The Shaftesbury Society and the National Society for Mentally Handicapped Children do this. St Dunstans is a training centre for men and women who were blinded in war service. This organisation helps them to find jobs and runs a training and holiday home. Also the Royal National Institute for the Blind has homes and schools for blind children and adults. It trains typists and has popularised the use of braille.

There are, of course, many other charities which help physically disabled, mentally handicapped children and adults, but the State still needs to provide more. Recently very seriously disabled people have been granted a special tax-free allowance of £4.80 a week. But this only covers about forty thousand people and, with the cost of living rising rapidly, it is nowhere near enough to provide for their special needs even when added to a disablement pension.

Old People

As people live longer more problems emerge. With the advances in medicine it is possible for old people merely to be kept alive even though that life consists of a vegetable-type existence with the loss of all faculties in a geriatric ward in hospital. Many people have expressed their belief that one should be able to choose one's right to die in such circumstances. However, such a situation could put a tremendous burden on medical staff and a patient's relatives.

Apart from special wards for old people in hospitals (geriatric wards) other services have been developed for the elderly. Old people can have special preventive treatment in day centres where they are given advice on the right type of food to eat. In most areas 'home helps' are available. These women go to old people's homes and help them with chores which, although they might be healthy, they cannot manage entirely on their own.

As most men now retire from full-time work at sixty-five and women at sixty, problems arise from coping with so much leisure time. The problem is aggravated if one is living on a fixed pension which is insufficient to cover rising costs of rent, heat, food, etc. Loneliness is another major problem. Supplementary benefit is available to pensioners on top of their regular old age pension, the amount varies according to their income and savings. Also pensioners, together with families who have low incomes, can often get a reduction in the amount of rates they pay. This is called the rate rebate scheme. Old people on supplementary benefit also get any increases in rent paid for them by the Ministry of Social Security.

For some pensioners, purpose-built Local Authority flats are available. For those who cannot really look after themselves and have no family, or a family who is reluctant to look after them, there are Local Authority homes. Many of these are bright, cheerful and well run. But for many old people they are looked on with fear and dread as they bring back memories of the old institution 'the workhouse' where one went to die in poverty and ignominy.

Most Boroughs now have free or reduced bus fares for old people as long as they use the buses out of the rush hour. Private enterprises such as launderers,

63 (*opposite*) Housing conditions in the early twentieth century. Many people have since been rehoused in council flats and houses; but in large cities housing is still a problem and overcrowded slums remain

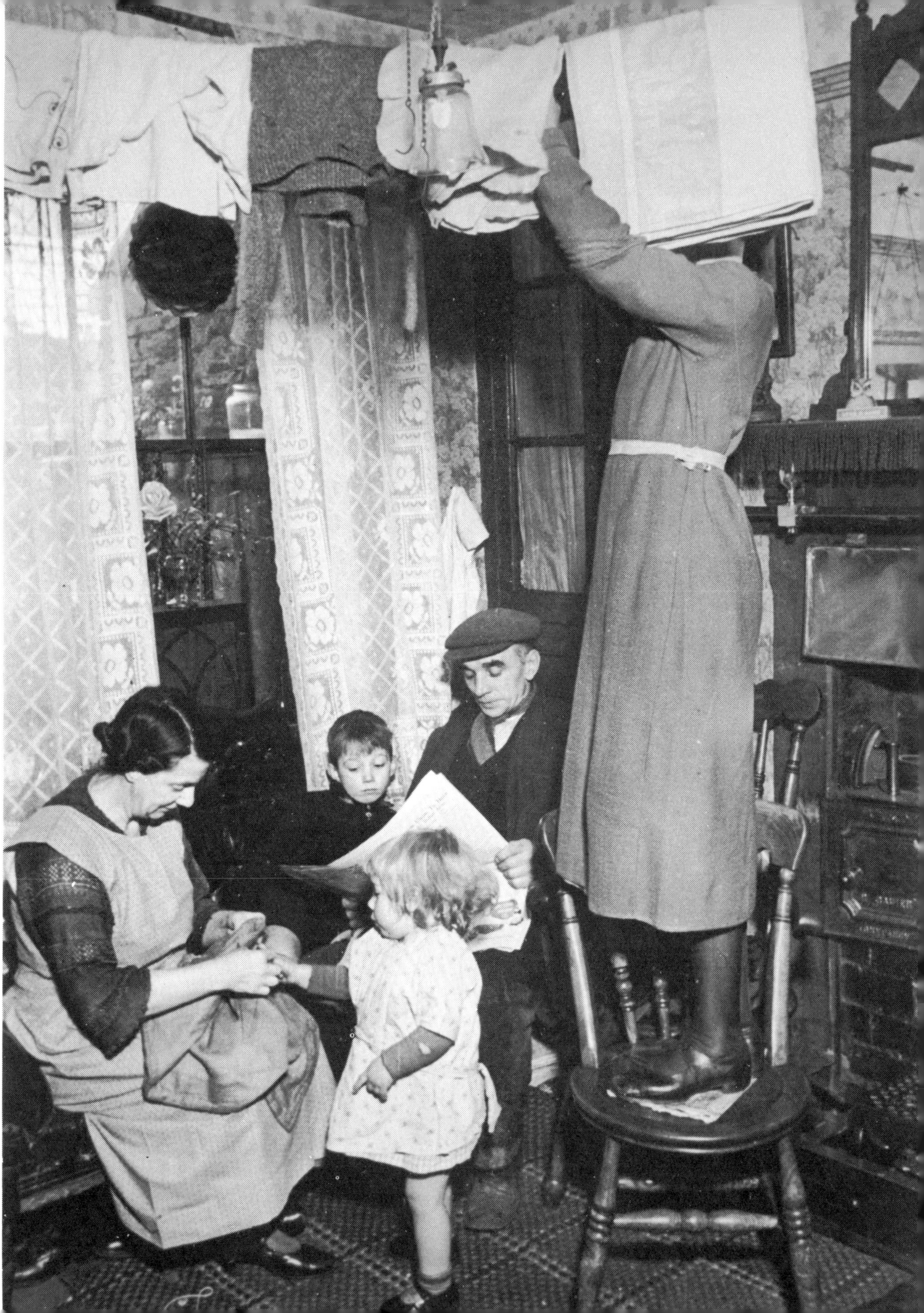

cleaners, cinemas also provide services at reduced rates for pensioners. But the grim fact still remains that many old people are still so poor they cannot make use of them.

Loneliness is a very acute problem for old people and one which the State has failed to deal with. Provision of clubs and centres for the elderly is really not enough. Also grouping old people's homes and flats together emphasises their isolation from the rest of the community. One successful voluntary organisation 'Task Force' is aware of the need for contact between old and young people. Task Force liases with local secondary schools and old people in a particular area. In school-time, school children, usually over the age of fifteen, visit old people, talk to them, do various jobs such as shopping, gardening and decorating. Another voluntary organisation, the Womens Royal Voluntary Service, provides a 'meals on wheels' service for old people. Each day they take hot cooked meals to old people who, for various reasons, cannot cook for themselves.

At the end of 1971 the problem of the really old was faced. For the over-eighties it meant that they were to get a pension for the first time. For $1\frac{1}{4}$ million eighty-year-olds and over, an extra 25p a week, on top of the normal pension was announced. Even so, as food prices were predicted to rise by at least 7 per cent during 1972 this hardly provides a comfortable existence for old people unless they have some kind of savings.

New Pressures of Urban Living

The growth of population, advances in technology, more leisure and unemployment affecting all social groups have proved a great strain on existing social services. The pressure of living in towns, changes in family structure and work patterns have revealed new needs. There is an increased demand for a new attitude towards mental illness. Alcoholism is recognised as an illness often caused by pressure of work or loneliness. Even so, much work in this field is done not so much by the conventional Health Service as by voluntary societies like Alcoholics Anonymous. The taking of drugs, although punishable by law, is nevertheless being recognised as an illness which desperately needs treatment. Venereal diseases are also treated within the Health Service. There are other problems too—all of which come within the province of the Welfare State and are far from being resolved. As in the nineteenth century, twentieth-century problems are largely created by the complexities of society and economic organisation.

In spite of the easier law regarding abortion and the growth of contraceptive advice there are still a large number of illegitimate births. Breakdown of marriages also causes social problems. Divorce has now been made easier, but there still remain the economic and emotional difficulties facing women who bring up children alone and men who are attempting to maintain more than one family. It would seem that the only solution to this is for maintainance allowances for children to come straight from the State so that a wife would not have to claim alimony from her husband through the courts. Widows also face problems if unprovided for, especially if they have young children or have to start to earn their own living at the age of forty or fifty. At the end of 1971 a gesture was made in this direction by the announcement of widows' pensions for women between the ages of forty and fifty.

Another problem, typical of the twentieth century, is the difficulty many people have in using leisure time. Of course, sometimes this leisure is enforced as a result of strike action, unemployment or redundancy. In such situations leisure time is seen as an extra burden along with the financial economies that often have to be made. On the other hand, in most occupations, working hours have become shorter, varying between thirty-five to forty-eight hours a week. Television and football are probably the most popular forms of entertainment—replacing radio and the cinema.

There is still the problem of open space. With the growth in population and density of housing, open spaces are gradually disappearing. Suburbia, especially around large cities, is spreading further and further into the countryside. High-rise flats mean that there is often nowhere for children to play. Many Local Authorities do provide and maintain parks and playgrounds, but such provision varies from one part of the country to another. It is interesting to remember that in the nineteenth century Octavia Hill and others stressed the importance of open spaces and waged long campaigns to get private gardens in London squares, such as Eaton Square, opened up for everyone's enjoyment, but many of these gardens still remain in private hands and are enjoyed only by a privileged minority.

Cultural Activities of the Welfare State
It has been recognised that certain forms of art and entertainment cannot exist unless given some kind of subsidy from the State. Largely these grants come from an organisation known as the Arts Council. Opera at the London Coliseum and Covent Garden receives a large grant, so do the major ballet companies, the Royal Ballet and the London Festival Ballet. It is mainly through financial help from the Arts Council that new concert halls, such as the Royal Festival Hall, are built. Experimental theatres can also obtain financial aid from the Arts Council, but this only provides a grant. Companies can only survive if they are also receiving help from a Local Authority and getting substantial box office takings. Some people object to the subsidy given to ballet and opera. They maintain that the companies are London based and that prices of seats are too high. On the other hand, many people feel the State should do much more to encourage the arts generally. Recently there has been a great campaign to stop wealthy foreigners buying famous paintings and taking them out of the country. Museums and galleries, traditionally free for the enjoyment of the general public, are now to charge an entry fee. This has caused a great deal of controversy. After all, the main purpose of a museum visit is not to try to see everything in one go, but to make many visits so that the collections can really be appreciated.

64 Slum children in the early twentieth century

The Changing Rôle of the Welfare State
We can see how the contemporary Welfare State has changed and evolved since the Second World War. Nineteenth-century attitudes and problems still remain. The State still does not provide everything, even in the way of basic services, as is shown by the number of voluntary charities which, by flag days and advertising campaigns in the press and on television, raise money for people in need.

To provide a better education system, more doctors, hospitals, houses, realistic pensions, family allowances, unemployment and supplementary benefit, the State, too, needs money invested in its welfare services in the same way as money is invested in industry and expensive space and defence programmes. People on higher incomes can afford to opt out of welfare services if they wish. They can buy a private education for their children, have private medical treatment and a more comfortable old age by joining a private pension scheme. It is argued that being able to choose this freedom is one of the rights of living in a democratic state. On the other hand, those on low incomes cannot make this choice. They have to take what the State provides. Often this is a second-class service, and although social services have developed and advanced considerably throughout the twentieth century there are still many gaps which private charity tries to fill.

The idea that everyone is entitled to minimum benefits has evolved very slowly. As we have seen, it is part of a centuries-old process developing out of private charities and ending up with State provision. On the way other rights have been established. The eighteenth century saw the winning of a legal battle which resulted in everyone being treated in the same way before the law. The establishment of political rights—the right to vote—was the main achievement of the nineteenth century (but not extended to women until the twentieth century). In the nineteenth century, too, we see the State starting to intervene in the fields of poverty, public health, housing, education, hours worked in industry. It was not until the twentieth century that the social rights of citizenship were really recognised. It was then that the foundations of the Welfare State were laid and its structure erected.

Today the functions of the Welfare State are much wider. As the State generally interferes and regulates political and economic life so there will be more done in other spheres. There is the problem of population control—only solved by effective contraception and more career opportunities for women. Most Local Authorities now support Family Planning Association Clinics, and some pay for the advice and contraceptives given to those who attend them. However, these are still mainly used by middle-class women, although they are open to all. There is also the problem of conserving the countryside, wildlife, old buildings which are all in danger of being destroyed by the 'needs' of modern society.

The Day-to-day Working of the Welfare State
The development of welfare services since 1945 has been most complex, covering an ever increasing range of problems. As a result the actual organisation and administration of the social services has grown. There are separate government Ministries, e.g. the Department of Health and Social Security; the Department of Education and Science; the Ministry of the Environment. These all cover a wide range of social services. There is a Minister for each. These are political appointments and change whenever there is a general election. The actual grinding work is carried out by a vast army of Civil Servants. Their job is to carry out whatever

the politicians decide. Besides the central government departments, many decisions are carried out at local government level. In fact the social services are financed directly from the government through taxation and, at local government level, from the rates.

County Councils and Boroughs provide health, cleansing and general environmental services. They also make provision for the old, children and families, provide schools and homes. Sometimes there is conflict between a Local Authority and the central government. This has been particularly evident recently when some Local Authorities have refused to carry out the Minister of Education's decision that there should be no more free milk provided in schools for children over seven. There has also been a lot of conflict over schemes for reorganising secondary education on comprehensive lines. Many of the conflicts involve money, as such projects as the building of new schools and hospitals are financed partly from the rates and partly from money from the central government.

There are many different authorities responsible for different areas of welfare. Many people who are in need and entitled to benefit just do not know where to go. In fact, during 1970 the *Guardian* newspaper revealed that many Post Offices did not have the necessary forms which people needed to claim different types of benefit, and counter clerks in Post Offices and officials in Social Security Offices were often unhelpful. Further confusion arises because some services are provided by the State, others by voluntary organisations. The local Post Office, library, town hall are places which should have information on various welfare services and where they can be obtained. Also in big towns there are Citizens Advice Bureaux which can advise on almost any problem. A particularly useful service provided by Citizens Advice Bureaux is a list of solicitors who participate in the government's Legal Aid scheme. Under this scheme anyone can have a consultation of half an hour with a solicitor for £1. Further advice can be given free or at reduced fees according to one's income.

Each Borough or County Borough has top officials who are responsible in different sectors of the social services. Sometimes their functions overlap. There is the Medical Officer of Health who is responsible for general health and environmental services. His job is to investigate and control infectious diseases, to arrange vaccination, immunisation and ambulance services. He and his department make sure that premises serving and selling food are up to standard. The Chief Education Officer and his staff are responsible for the general supervision of schools and colleges. They also have to make arrangements for handicapped children and supervise the school medical and school meals service. Very important is the Children's Officer who looks after children in need of help. This often means dealing with a whole family especially if the parents, for various reasons, are unable to look after their children. The Children's Officer arranges for children to go into Local Authority Homes and also organises adoption of children. The Children's Department of any Borough usually works very closely with voluntary associations whose aim is to help children in distress. Another

65 A new London primary school. Note the contrast with the children in the previous picture

important officer is the Housing Manager. He is in charge of housing which belongs to the County Borough or Borough Council. He has to see that the houses are maintained in good order. Sometimes he has to act like a welfare officer when feuds between neighbours need settling or families have got behind with their rent.

    These are only just a few of the administrators of the social services at local level. Each department has many people working in it and a locally elected committee which is unpaid and advises on policy. Even so, as the rôle of the Welfare State expands, so it becomes increasingly more difficult for people to know exactly where to go for help. Many are confused by forms they have to fill in. Others are too proud to ask for help for fear of being branded as 'scroungers' or 'malingerers'. For some people the Welfare State hardly exists—particularly the 'down and outs' we still see sleeping in bus shelters, railway stations or park benches because they have nowhere else to go.

Further reading
K. Coats and R. Silburn, *Poverty: The Forgotten Englishmen* (Pelican)
W. A. Robson and B. Crick, *The Future of the Social Services* (Pelican)
H. Gavron, *The Captive Wife* (Pelican)
J. Mitchell, *Women's Estate* (Pelican)
P. Willmott, *Consumer's Guide to the British Social Services* (Pelican)

Chronology

It has taken over three hundred years for the State to take responsibility for welfare services. The first important landmark was the Poor Law of 1601. Before that the underprivileged had to rely on private charity. It was not until the nineteenth century that the State gradually came to provide skeleton services in the field of factory reform, public health, provision for the poor, education and housing. A more comprehensive service was established in the twentieth century. Even so there is still plenty of room for charitable efforts.

1601 POOR LAW ACT
Each parish was made responsible for its own poor. Everyone had to pay a poor rate to maintain the poor. Outdoor relief was given to those who were unable to work through no fault of their own. In some areas Houses of Correction were set up for those who refused to work.

1662 ACT OF SETTLEMENT
Each parish was made responsible for maintaining the poor who were born there. People who had not found work within forty days in a new parish could be sent back to their old one.

1795 SPEENHAMLAND SYSTEM
Berkshire magistrates decide to supplement labourers' wages according to the price of bread. This system of allowances in-aid-of-wages spread rapidly into other counties.

1819 Peel's Factory Act limited work in textile factories for children under nine.

1833 The State made a first grant of £33,000 to the Voluntary Schools.

1833 Factory Act. Children under the age of 13 could only work nine hours a day, young persons between 13 and 18 years were to work a twelve-hour day. The Act applied to textile factories only, inspectors were appointed to see that it was carried out.

1834 THE NEW POOR LAW
The old system of outdoor relief is abolished. Relief is now to be given through workhouses.

1840 A select committee investigates the health of towns.

1841 Earliest model dwellings built.

1842 Mines Act forbids women and boys under ten from working underground in the mines.

1842 Report on the sanitary conditions of the labouring population of Great Britain.
Edwin Chadwick reveals shattering statistics about the wastage of life due to inadequate housing and public health facilities.

1844 Factory Act restricts the working hours of women and young people to 10½ hours a day.

1848 PUBLIC HEALTH ACT
Gives opportunity to towns to appoint their own Medical Officer of Health and set up local Boards of Health.

1862 The Peabody Trust is established for 'the poor of London'.

1864 Octavia Hill starts her housing work.

1866 Local Authorities are forced to employ sanitation inspectors.

1870 Education Act which compels Local Authorities to provide elementary schools where there are no suitable voluntary schools.

1872 Public Health Act makes it compulsory for Local Authorities to appoint Medical Officers of Health.

1875 The Cross Act gives powers to Local Authorities to pull down slums and rebuild.

1875 Public Health Act sets up administrative machinery for a health service. Local Authorities could now make by-laws regulating buildings. Cellar dwellings are finally banned.

1880 Attendance at school is made compulsory.

1891 Elementary education is made free.

1897 Workmen's Compensation Act. Employers are made responsible for workers injured in their factories.

1902 Education Act abolishes School Boards and sets up Local Authorities. Secondary education is provided in some areas.

1906 Free school meals for poor children are introduced.

1907 A free school medical service begins.

1909 Lloyd George introduces graduated income tax to pay for old age pensions.

1911 The National Insurance Act: workers start to contribute to an insurance scheme against sickness. Some free medical treatment is provided for certain categories of workers.

1918 The Fisher Act raises the school leaving age to fourteen.

1931 Unemployment relief only given after a Means Test which is applied to all wage earners in a family.

1942 Sir William Beveridge recommends a comprehensive national insurance system.

1944 BUTLER EDUCATION ACT reorganises education into primary, secondary and further education. The school leaving age is raised to 15 years. The eleven plus exam is introduced.

1946 THE NATIONAL HEALTH ACT provides a completely free medical service for everyone.

1946 National Insurance Act makes everyone contribute towards an insurance fund. From this fund they can now draw unemployment pay, pensions in old age, family allowances and maternity benefit.

1947 The National Assistance Act provides financial help for anyone who is able to prove their need.

1963 Robbins Report on higher education.

1967 Plowden Report on primary schools.

1968 Seebohm Report urges social workers to treat the family as a unit and not deal with its various difficulties in separate departments.

1969 Maud Report on the Health Service recommends large multi-purpose health centres and amalgamation of small regional hospital boards.

1971 Welfare starts to cost more, prescription charges are increased, spectacles and dental treatment are no longer free; school meals cost more; free milk in schools is abolished.

Index

Numbers in **bold type** refer to the figure numbers of the illustrations.

Arts Council, 85
Ashley, Lord, 39

Badging the poor, 12
Boer War, 44
Bentham, Jeremy, 17
Bevan, Aneurin, 72
Beveridge, William, 51, 65
Black Death, 9
British and Foreign Society, 34, 42
Boards of Guardians, 20
Booth, Charles, 45, 48

Census, *1861*, 29, 30
Chadwick, Edwin, **16**
    Poor Law, 19–20
    Health of towns, 24–26
Charity school movement, 13
Child Poverty Action Group, 28
Children's Acts, 57, 67, 68
Cholera, 25; **17**
Colleges of Education, 71
Common Lodging Houses Act, 31; **18**
Comprehensive schools, 69; **54**

Education Act *1870*, 41; *1902*, 43; *1918*, 56; *1944*, 69
Educational Priority Areas, 71

Factory Act *1833*, 37; *1844*, 38
Family Allowances Act, 65
Friendly Societies, 21–22; **15**

General Strike, 57
Gilds, 8
Gilbert's Act, 14

Hadlow Report, 57
Hazelwood Schools, 34
Health and Morals of Apprentices Act, 36
Hill, Octavia, 33, 85; **25**
Hospitals, 74; **51**
Housing, Slums, 24–30, 60; **20, 37, 48**
    Workers' houses, 32, 33; **23, 24**
    Council houses, 59–60
    New housing schemes, 75; **59, 60, 62**

Immunisation, 64
Improved Industrial Dwellings Company, 32
Industrial Revolution, 14; **30, 31**

Labour Exchanges, 51; **42**
Lloyd George, David, 49, 51, 52; **39, 40**

Local Government Board, 24
Lowe, Robert, 41

Means Test, 59
Monasteries, 8; **1, 2**
Monitorial system, 34, 35; **26**
Mines Act, *1842*, 39
Ministry of Social Security, 66

National Assistance Board, 66
National Society, 34, 42
National Health Service, 72
National Insurance, 51, 66
Newcastle Commission, 41
New Towns, 33, 77
New universities, 71
Nuisance Removal Acts, 31

Old people, 49, 66, 82
Open University, 71
Outdoor relief, 11
Overseers of the poor, 11

Pauper children, 11
Payment by results, 41, 43
Peabody Trust, 32
Peasants' Revolt, 9
Pensions, 66; **41**
Plowden Report, 71
Poor Laws *1388*, 10; *1601*, 11; *1834*, 19
Poor Law Commission *1905–1909*, 48
Poor Laws, Reorganisation of, *1929*, 57
Primary Schools, 71; **65**
Private Charity, 10, 11, 12, 13, 81; **4, 7**
Public Health Acts *1848*, 25; *1871*, *1875*, 27–28
Pupil Teachers, 40

Ragged Schools, 35; **27**
Rathbone, Eleanor, 59, 66
Rationing, 63, 64; **50**
Remand Homes, 54
Rent Acts, 76
Revised Code, 41
Rowntree Seebohm, 42, 46, 47, 78

Sanitary Conditions of the Labouring Poor, Report, 25
School Boards, 42
School Meals, 54, 64
School Medical Service, 54; **58**
Second World War, 62
Settlement Acts, 12
'Shelter', 77

Shuttleworth, James Kay, 40, 41
Simon, John, 27
Southwood Smith, 24
Speenhamland System, 16
Statute of Artificers, 11

'Task Force', 84
Ten Hours Act, 38
Toynbee Hall, 45

Unemployment, 51, 58, 66; **47, 52, 61**

Unemployment Assistance Board, 58
Unemployment insurance, 51
Utilitarianism, 17
University settlements, 44

Voluntary societies, 34, 42, 81

Waterlow, Sydney, 32
War socialism, 62
Workhouses, 20, 21; **11, 14, 36**
Webb, Sidney and Beatrice, 48